50 Real Ghost S

Spirits In The Shadows

By MJ Wayland

"Maybe all the people who say ghosts don't exist are just afraid to admit that they do." – Michael Ende, 'The Neverending Story'

Paperback published Halloween 2023
ISBN: 9798864292341

Copyright © 2023 MJ Wayland
All Artwork Copyright © 2023 L.Jeffrey

All rights reserved. No part of this publication may be reproduced, stored in a retrieval system, or transmitted, in any form or by any means without the prior written permission of the publisher, nor be otherwise circulated in any form of binding or cover other than that in which it is published and without a similar condition being imposed on the subsequent purchaser.

Published by Ghost Lantern

Author website
www.mjwayland.com

Artist website
https://unseely.com

Contents

Foreword 5
The Eyeless Spectre 7
The Haunting of the Old Hotel 9
The Spectral Lady Road Ghost 10
Messages from Beyond 13
Whispers in the Walls 14
The Curse of the Opal Ring 16
Noisy Ghosts 18
Flaming Orb 19
Phantom Boy of Chillingham Castle 21
Knocking Phantom 23
The Black Dust 25
Nine Ladies Stone Circle Elemental 27
Business Centre Ghost 28
The Pretty Lady 29
Telephone Call from Beyond 31
The Silent Guide 32
The Old Railway Tunnel 35
The Black Swan Ghost 37
Ever-Present Companions 39
Unwanted Gift 41
It Followed Me Home 44
The Horfield Common Horror 46
Tin Mine Ghost 50
Thundridge Church 52
Woodhead Pass Lights 55
Haunting Memories of Repton School 58
Smugglers back from the Dead? 60
Dad was never the same 62
Strange Stories from the Old Vic 64
Jacobite Spirits Still Linger? 66
Haunted Holiday 68
A Jinn or a ghost? 70
The Curse 72
Westbury Swimming Pool 74
Who was Bloody Mary? 76
Grandad's Promise: An Unseen, Unbreakable Bond 80

The Thing 82
My Hell in a Haunted House 84
Derry's Phantom Field: A Ghostly Encounter 87
A Life of Experiences 88
Haunted Caravan 90
Burning Man of RAF Woodbridge 93
4:00pm 95
From the Author 98
About the Artist 99

Foreword

"The boundaries which divide Life from Death are at best shadowy and vague. Who shall say where the one ends, and where the other begins?" - Edgar Allan Poe

As you delve into the dimly lit passages of 50 Real Ghost Stories 3, prepare to journey into the ethereal realm of spirits and spectres. I, MJ Wayland, your trusted guide, welcome you on this spectral journey of fright and fascination, filled with tales that challenge the very concept of reality as we know it.

Prepare to meet the "Eyeless Spectre," one of the most unnerving ghost stories ever shared with me, unfolding within the hallowed halls of a Liverpool school. Venture into the creaking corridors and haunting histories of "The Haunting of the Old Hotel," a tale that reminds us that remnants of the past can refuse to fade away. Traverse the chilling path of "The Spectral Lady Road Ghost," a tale that paints a road less travelled with shades of the uncanny, a spectral journey situated perilously close to the infamously haunted Berry Pomeroy Castle.

Over many years, I have dedicated my life to the investigation of these spectral narratives, and it is my honour to present to you this collection of stories. Each one is a true account, delivered to me from a real witness, and has been meticulously curated, analysed, and beautifully retold to preserve the authenticity and raw emotion they possess. As I have mentioned in my previous books, real ghost stories often do not have a conclusion; they refuse to offer a neatly packaged ending. There is no rhyme or reason to these spectral accounts - this is real life, and real life seldom follows a script.

My interest in the supernatural is not merely a product of morbid curiosity, but rather a quest for understanding - an exploration into the strange, seemingly inexplicable phenomena that push the boundaries of our known reality. Ghosts, spirits, spectres, apparitions - whatever term you prefer - serve as symbols of the mysteries that lie beyond our tangible world, offering hints and whispers of the ultimate unknown: what comes after life as we know it.

This third instalment continues to tread upon the eerie, uncanny territories of the unseen, the unheard, the unexplained. It's a meeting point of human fear and fascination, a demonstration of our collective obsession with the spectral. Within these pages, you will find tales of lost souls wandering in the twilight between life and death, haunted places whispering stories of centuries gone by, and inexplicable occurrences that will make you question your very understanding of reality.

But why do we crave such narratives? Is it the thrill of the fright, the titillation of terror, the allure of the unknown? Or do these stories resonate with us on a deeper, more primordial level, tapping into our collective subconscious, echoing the universal question: What becomes of us after our last breath escapes our lips?

As you turn the pages of this book, let yourself be swept away by the haunting symphony of these spectral accounts. Embrace the shiver down your spine, the quickening of your heartbeat, the silence that falls around you. Remember, dear reader, each story holds a deeper truth - an echo of human emotions, fears, desires, and the ultimate mystery of existence itself.

Whether you're a sceptic seeking answers or a believer eager for validation, I invite you to suspend your disbelief, open your mind, and allow yourself to traverse the dim corridors of the afterlife with me. You are about to embark on an expedition to the other side of the veil, to where the line between the living and the dead blurs.

Welcome, dear reader, to the spectral symphony of "50 Real Ghost Stories 3." I hope you find as much fascination, intrigue, and shivers down the spine within these pages as I did in the many hours spent gathering these stories.

Let's step into the shadows together...

MJ Wayland

The Eyeless Spectre

I've got a tale that might give you a shiver, one that dates back to my school days.

Our school was one of those old Victorian school buildings that had been converted in the 1960s very unsuccessfully so there was a blend of history and modern extensions and wall separators.

I was about ten when I first saw him. It was a rainy afternoon, and I was in the classroom, lost in some boring lesson. My eyes wandered to the back of the room, and there, in the corner, was a boy I'd never seen before.

He was about my age, dressed in an old-fashioned uniform, the kind you see in black and white photos. But the most startling thing was his face. Where his eyes should've been, there were just dark, empty sockets.

The sight froze me in my tracks. I blinked, rubbed my eyes, but when I looked back, he was still there, standing silently. Nobody else seemed to notice him. I was terrified, but also strangely fascinated.

I was in that classroom for about two years, and I saw that boy a several times, always in the same corner of the room, always silent, always watching. It got to the point where I was scared to go to school, scared to turn my head and see him there. But I never told anyone, thinking they'd laugh it off, say I was seeing things.

Years passed, and I left school, but the memory of the eyeless boy stayed with me. He still appears in my dreams, standing in the corner, watching me with his sightless eyes.

Recently, at a school reunion, I gathered the courage to ask my old mates if they'd ever seen anything unusual at school. To my surprise, a couple of them recalled similar encounters, confirming my own experiences, and we wondered if anyone else had reported it, so we reached out to our old teachers through Facebook.

We were surprised when old Mr. Higgins actually replied, he told us that there had been rumours about a ghost boy when the school first opened, but nothing had been reported in years. While he taught at the school, he never saw the boy but there were always rumours in the staffroom that a particular pupil had seen a ghost. Usually, they thought it was a prank of some kind.

I felt reassured that others had seen the boy, but I still carry the trauma, the eyeless boy still remains in my thoughts and sometimes in my nightmares.

The Haunting of the Old Hotel

The building I live in was once an old hotel, known for its grandeur and elegance in the 1920s. In the 1990s, the rooms were knocked through and sold off as flats (apartments).

From the moment I moved in, peculiar things began to happen. I'd hear hushed whispers, the subtle sound of old music echoing through the hallways late at night, and an inexplicable cold spot in my living room. I thought it might be the neighbours or kids messing around in the hallway.

One night, however, things took a chilling turn. I was awakened from a deep sleep by a sense of unease. The air was heavy, and the moonlight streaming through the window barely illuminated the room. In the far corner, I noticed a shadowy figure, standing still, seemingly watching me. The figure was tall, wearing what appeared to be a bellhop uniform of yesteryears. I didn't know if I was dreaming, but then I felt a chill on my face.

A wave of fear washed over me as I locked eyes with the shadowy figure. It didn't move, it just stood there, silent and imposing. Suddenly, an overpowering smell filled the room, a stench so strong and foul - it was undeniably the smell of tar or asphalt. I covered my nose, my eyes watering, and when I looked back, the figure was gone.

Sleep eluded me for the rest of the night. The following day, I asked the building manager if there had been any strange occurrences in the past. Apparently, the flat had been rented out a few times and people didn't stay long.

The shadowy figure never appeared again, but the memory of that night lingered, casting a shadow over my once peaceful flat. Even though I was frightened, I chose to stay, constantly worried that it might appear again in the middle of the night.

The Spectral Lady Road Ghost

I've been a long-haul trucker for more than a decade, spending countless hours navigating the winding, often lonely, roads of Devon and England under the cover of night. I've seen weird stuff, soldiers hiding under bushes (a military exercise), cars flipped over at the side of the road, and even a heard of horses galloping at night down the road. Yet, there's one journey that still haunts my dreams, a chilling encounter on a frigid winter night that has left an indelible mark on my memory.

I was making my way through the quiet, rural roads on the outskirts of Totnes, Devon, the blackness of the night pierced only by the glow of my truck's headlights. The road was desolate, and the air had a chill that seeped into the cabin. It was then that I saw her, a spectral figure standing by the roadside. She was dressed in an old-fashioned white gown that seemed to glow ethereally against the backdrop of the dark night. Her face, pale and almost translucent, was illuminated by the harsh glare of the headlights.

I remember how fast my heartbeat when I saw her, I slammed on the brakes and quickly looked at the rear-view mirror. I was expecting to see her again, but she had vanished. Shaken but rational, I dismissed the apparition as a figment of my fatigued mind playing tricks on me.

A few weeks later, I found myself back on the same route, this time with my partner, Sarah, accompanying me. As we approached the spot that had been the stage for my eerie encounter, I couldn't help but share the story with her. She laughed, telling me that the ghost was probably lack of sleep or an overactive imagination.

But just as she was dismissing my tale, the woman materialised once more. Her spectral figure glowed in the glare of my headlights, standing at the very same spot by the road. Sarah let out a terrified scream as I swerved the truck, our hearts pounding in unison. But when we dared to look back, the ghostly figure had disappeared once more. We both got out of the truck, shining our torches up the road and nothing could be found. The road in question, the Totnes Road off the A385 is almost singular, it's that tight of a road with high hedges and tall grass and wildflowers. There was nowhere anyone could have hidden that night. We noticed a car in the distance approaching so we set off.

Both rattled and perplexed by our shared experience, we pulled into a local pub upon reaching the next town. Over a round of drinks, we shared our story with the locals, hoping they could shed some light on our eerie encounter. An old man, a lifelong resident, shared a tale from the 18th century about a young woman named Elizabeth. She was said to have waited on that very spot for her lover to return from war, dressed in her best white gown. Sadly, he never returned, and she died of a broken heart, forever waiting by the road.

I'll be honest, the story shook me to the core. I haven't mustered the courage to drive the Totnes to Berry Pomeroy route again. The fear that the spectral figure might reappear and the uncertainty of what it might mean for me continues to haunt me.

Another observer reached out to the author, having also seen the White Lady of Berry Pomeroy while on Totnes Road. The lady told me the following incident.

About thirty-six years ago, I was travelling home on the Totnes Road walking from St Mary's church to my Gran's house just passed the old cemetery.

As I was strolling down the deserted road at night when I caught a glimpse of something unusual out of the corner of my eye. A little way off the road, I saw a figure, a woman dressed in a long, old-fashioned white gown. She was standing there, her face pale and almost glowing in the moonlight. She seemed to be looking at the road but couldn't see me!

A sense of unease washed over me, but I found myself rooted to the spot, transfixed by the sight. Then she simply vanished, as though she had been a mere illusion. I blinked, not trusting my own eyes. She was there one moment and gone the next.
With my heart pounding in my chest, I forced my legs to move and hurried along, eager to reach the safety of my Gran's house. Once

inside I ran to Gran and told her about my strange experience. She told me of the story of Elizabeth, who apparently used to wait for her lover on the road, sadly he died never returned from the Boer War and she died of a broken heart, her spirit said to linger on, forever waiting by the road.

Beyond the Castle
I checked the notes of local ghost and folklore expert Theo Brown and searched countless books and newspapers for other sightings of 'Elizabeth' but found nothing. The fact that two independent accounts, from my files and several years apart, suggest that there is indeed a once unreported phantom woman appearing on a desolate road in an old-fashioned white gown.

Berry Pomeroy is a village already well-known for its haunted castle, a place teeming with ghost stories and eerie legends. The castle has long been the centrepiece of local lore, with its tales of ghostly apparitions and strange occurrences. However, these new accounts indicate that the haunting of Berry Pomeroy might extend beyond the castle's ancient walls to the surrounding roads.

Both the stories, while different in their circumstances, add weight to the idea that the road leading to Berry Pomeroy might be just as haunted as the castle itself. The spectral figure of Elizabeth, forever waiting for her lover by the road, has become a lingering spectre, casting a haunting shadow over the area. Therefore, in Berry Pomeroy, both the journey and the destination hold the potential for a chilling encounter with the past.

Messages from Beyond

My dear husband Edward passed away recently. Edward and I shared a love that spanned over six decades. He was my confidant, my companion, my rock. Losing him felt like losing a part of my soul. Our house, once filled with laughter and love, had fallen silent.

A few weeks after his passing, strange things began to happen. It started with faint sounds - footsteps in the hallway, a soft humming of our favourite tune, the same one he would hum while gardening. I would smell his cologne, a woody, comforting scent, wafting through the house at random times.

One evening, as I sat in Edward's favourite side of the settee reading a book, I distinctly felt a weight settle next to me. It was the same familiar warmth I used to feel when Edward would sit by my side. My heart pounded as I turned to look, but there was nothing there, just the lingering imprint of someone having been seated there.

I was startled, but not frightened. Somehow, these occurrences gave me a sense of peace, as though Edward was still with me, watching over me.

One night, the most incredible thing happened. I was jolted awake by the sound of Edward's voice. It was crystal clear, as if he was right next to me. He said, "Margaret, my love, don't worry. I'm still here with you." I turned on the bedside lamp, half expecting to see him there, but the room was empty.

I've come to believe that Edward is indeed with me, even in death. While our daughters say it might have been a dream, I feel Edwards was offering me comfort when his loss felt too immense.

People might think I'm an old woman losing her senses, but I know what I've experienced. The ghostly occurrences are a testament to our bond, a bond that even death couldn't break.

Whispers in the Walls

I live in an old house converted into flats (apartments) many years ago. The walls are paper thin, so often I think the noises I hear are from the neighbours, but my experiences go far beyond that.

For years I had lived in shared accommodation with my son Tommy, and after a long wait we were given keys to a newly developed flat, what a relief to have a place to call our own. I didn't realise when we moved in, that the house was already occupied, but not by the living.

From the moment we moved in, strange things began to happen. It started subtly, with little things going missing – Tommy's toys, my keys, a cup of tea I was certain I'd just made. Then they'd reappear in the oddest places, like under the sink or in the bathtub. I blamed it on the stress of moving, the sleep deprivation that comes with being a young mum. But as the weeks went on, the happenings grew stranger.

One chilly night, I was woken up by a soft lullaby that seemed to be wafting through the house. It was a tune I didn't recognise, but it was unmistakably a lullaby. Puzzled, I got up to investigate, thinking it might be a neighbour or maybe a toy accidentally switched on.

The sound led me to Tommy's room. As I approached, the lullaby got louder. I pushed open the door, my heart pounding in my chest. The room was dark, but for the faint moonlight streaming through the window. Tommy was sound asleep, but the lullaby was still playing.

In the corner of the room, I saw a figure. A woman, transparent and dressed in an old-fashioned dress, was rocking back and forth in the rocking chair we'd never used, humming the lullaby. She looked up at me with sad, knowing eyes, then faded away, leaving only the echo of her song and a sudden chill in the room.

I was terrified, but I noticed Tommy seemed peaceful, undisturbed by the spectral presence. Over the following months, I heard the ghostly woman humming her lullaby a few more times. While in the bathroom one night I saw her shadowy figure passing in the hallway. I look back at these experiences and realise for some reason I wasn't that scared.

One day, I mentioned the occurrences to an elderly neighbour. She grew quiet, then told me about a young woman who had lived in my house in the 1940s. She was a single mother, like me, who had struggled to make ends meet. Tragically, she had died young, leaving her little boy behind.

After hearing this, my fear turned into a strange kind of understanding. I didn't feel alone anymore in my struggles. Instead, I felt a connection to this woman from the past who, even in death, was trying to comfort her child and perhaps mine too.

The Curse of the Opal Ring

I run a small second-hand stall in the bustling Portobello Market in London. I've always had a knack for finding hidden treasures among the discarded items, but one particular piece brought more than I bargained for – an opal ring, glimmering with spectral colours.

From the moment I bought the ring I had a run of bad luck. My once busy stall began to lose customers, takings were down and items began to break inexplicably. One morning while packing the van for the market I sprained my ankle and couldn't get to the stall. I'm usually a cheerful, happy person but after all this bad luck I felt sad, unease and even dread when waking up in the morning.

Maybe it was the stress, but I couldn't sleep but when I finally did manage to drift off I was haunted by strange nightmares. In my dreams I could see young woman dressed in 1960s clothing, her eyes filled with sorrow. Over the days she began to reach out to me, pleading, pointing towards the ring I had placed on my bedside table.

One morning, I woke up to find the opal ring wasn't on the table where I had left it. Instead, it was resting on my pillow, its luminescent stones glowing eerily in the early morning light. I was sure I hadn't moved it in my sleep, and there was no one else in my apartment.

I took the ring to a local spiritualist church, before I had even said a word, one of the women there said, "who is the 1960s girl you've brought with you?"

I felt faint and over a cup of tea told of the spiritualist about the issues I had experience. She told me the ring once belonged to Eleanor – the 1960s girl. She had owned the ring and died tragically young in a scooter accident on the way to Brighton. Grief-stricken, her fiancé had cursed the ring, blaming it for her untimely death.

I didn't know what to believe, with this knowledge, I felt a strange mix of fear and empathy. I began to understand the woman in my dreams, her sorrow, and her connection to the ring. I decided I had to break the curse, not just for my sake, but for Eleanor's too.

On the advice of the spiritualist, I conducted a simple releasing ceremony. I lit a white candle, placed the ring next to it, and spoke aloud, "Eleanor, your pain is acknowledged. I release you from this ring. Find peace and let peace return to me."

That night, I slept without nightmares. The next morning, I woke up to find the ring back on the table, its stones dull and lifeless. From that day forward, my run of bad luck ended. My stall began to thrive again, and my life returned to normal. Whether you believe my story or not doesn't matter to me, I still have the opal ring and it is a reminder of the experiences and connection I had with Eleanor, and how it stands as a symbol of release and peace for both of us.

Did you hear that?

Noisy Ghosts

My name is Mike. I've recently moved into an old house in the countryside. For the first few weeks, everything was incredibly peaceful. However, things started to change, and I began experiencing strange occurrences.

One night, I heard a loud crash in the kitchen. I rushed in only to find pots and pans scattered all over the floor. The following day, the same thing happened, but this time, it was in the living room. Books were thrown off the shelves, picture frames were knocked over, and even the couch seemed to have been moved as if someone had been pushing it.

The incidents became increasingly eerie. I started to hear whispers, as if someone was speaking directly into my ear. I found cold spots around the house in places that shouldn't be cold. Once, I saw a shadow move across the wall when there was no one there to cast it.

I decided to investigate this situation. I picked up a book from the library that delved into the paranormal, particularly about ghosts and similar entities. The book suggested that I might be dealing with a poltergeist. I'm not sure what to do next, but I'm determined to stay.

This is my home now, and if necessary, I'm prepared to share it with a ghost.

Flaming Orb

Growing up in the rural outskirts of Sheffield, we often found ourselves exploring the woods near our home. The woods were a place of adventure and curiosity, but they also held an eerie secret – an old brick shed, the only remnant of a once-thriving workhouse that had since been converted into a hospital.

The old brick shed was our secret clubhouse, a place we'd escape to after school, telling ghost stories and daring each other to venture inside. Despite its dilapidated state, there was an unmistakable aura around it, a feeling of unease and dirtiness – the whole place felt grimy far beyond than what it looked.

Over time, we started experiencing strange occurrences. Unexplained cold spots in the middle of a summer afternoon, shadows dancing at the corners of our eyes, and an overwhelming sense of being watched. The thrill of fear, the allure of the unknown kept us coming back, despite the growing unease.

One day, we decided to experiment with a Ouija board. It was an old one, borrowed from my friend's attic, its wooden surface worn, and letters faded. We gathered around it in the shed, our hearts beating with anticipation and fear. As our hands touched the planchette, the atmosphere seemed to shift, the air growing denser, the shadows deepening. Although it was a summer's day, I felt as if the forest became darker, and within the shed, the gloom spread.

We asked questions, silly ones at first, like "Is there anyone here with us?" and "What's your name?" The planchette moved, spelling out answers that sent chills down our spines. The room seemed to grow colder, the silence outside becoming deafening.

Suddenly, one of us, Bradley, who was standing by the entrance, let out a gasp. We turned to see him pointing upwards, his face pale as a ghost.

Following his gaze, we were stunned to see a floating flame above the shed. It hovered there, a burning orb casting an otherworldly glow on the dilapidated brick structure.

We ran, leaving the Ouija board behind, our hearts pounding in our chests. We didn't stop until we reached our homes, the image of the floating flame burned into our minds. The next day, we returned to the shed, expecting to find the Ouija board where we'd left it. But it was gone.

We stopped visiting the old brick shed after that incident. The memories of the floating flame and the ominous Ouija board were too much to handle. We were just children, unprepared for the eerie reality we had stumbled upon.

Phantom Boy of Chillingham Castle

My name's Howard, a bit of an enthusiast for all things historical and paranormal. My story takes place during a visit to Chillingham Castle, renowned as one of the most haunted places in Britain.

Upon my arrival, I was met with a less than warm welcome. The castle staff seemed indifferent, bordering on rude. I was disappointed, but I'd come a long way, and the allure of spending a night in a haunted castle was too enticing to turn down.

I was lodged in a quaint room with heavy drapes and antique furniture. It had an old-world charm, but there was an air of unease, an undercurrent of energy that felt off. As night fell, the castle grew eerily silent.

At around 3 am, I woke up with a start. The room was darker than I remembered, and the curtains at the window were rustling, despite the window being shut. My heart pounded in my chest as I saw a small, dark figure walking around the room.

It moved with an eerie grace, its steps barely making a sound. It seemed to be searching for something, never acknowledging my presence. I was terrified, my body frozen in fear. I did the only thing I could think of - I pulled the sheets over my head, praying for morning to come quickly.

Underneath the covers, I could hear the faint rustling of movement, the hushed whispers of an unseen presence. I must have eventually drifted off to sleep, because the next thing I remember was the morning light streaming through the open curtains.

I sat up, looking around the room. Everything was as it had been when I'd gone to sleep. There was no sign of the small, dark figure that had stalked my room the night before. I was left questioning if it had been real, or if it had just been a product of my imagination, fuelled by the eerie atmosphere of the castle.

The memory of that night at Chillingham Castle remains with me. The rudeness of the staff, the eerie silence of the castle at night, and the small, dark figure wandering in my room. Was it a dream? Or a spectral encounter? I may never know, but the haunting image of that small, dark figure remains etched in my memory.

Radiant Boy Returns?
One of the most famous ghost stories of Chillingham Castle is that of the Radiant Boy. While well reported in Victorian times since the refurbishment of the Castle he has been hardly reported. Another real-life experience was sent to me about the castle that also included a possible encounter of the Radiant Boy!

I found myself drawn to the castle's old dungeon. The guide said it was a place of chilling tales and cruel history, a place that had seen immense suffering and despair. The moment I stepped inside, I could feel a tangible change in the atmosphere that sent shivers down my spine.

There, in the dimly lit room, a figure caught my eye. It was the apparition of a small boy, no older than ten, wearing a blue doublet, common clothing of the 16th century. His face, pale and melancholic, contrasted starkly with the vibrancy of his clothes.

As I stood, locked, looking at the ghost a wave of dread washed over me. Yet, I felt an inexplicable pull towards the boy. As I cautiously moved closer, the air grew colder, and a silence so deep enveloped the room that it felt as if time itself had paused.

The boy seemed oblivious to my presence; his gaze fixated on something unseen. Then, he turned, his eyes meeting mine, and in that moment, I felt a surge of emotions – fear, sadness, and an aching loneliness. Then, as quickly as he appeared, he vanished, leaving nothing but an echo of his presence and a lingering chill.

Shaken, I left the dungeon, the image of the boy in the blue doublet etched in my memory. I later learned from the castle's guide about chilling tales of a young boy who was reportedly seen in the dungeon, thought to be the spirit of a child who had died tragically within the castle's walls centuries ago.

Knocking Phantom

When I was a child, we lived in a lovely old house on the outskirts of York, England. It was a grand Victorian home with creaky wooden floors, high ceilings, and ornate mouldings. The walls held secrets of the past, and the rooms echoed with memories. It was a house filled with laughter, warmth, and a slightly mischievous ghost.

The strange occurrences started when I was about seven. It was a bright, sunny afternoon, and I was in my room, engrossed in a book. The room was adorned with pastel-coloured wallpaper and overlooked our sprawling garden. Suddenly, I heard a distinct knock on the window. I looked out, expecting to see a bird or maybe a friend playing a prank, but there was nothing. The garden outside was empty, the trees still, and the flowers swaying gently with the breeze.

I shrugged it off, thinking it was just the house settling or perhaps my imagination playing tricks on me. But then it happened again. And again. Always three knocks, clear and distinct, always during the day, and always when I was alone in the room.

The knocks became a regular occurrence, almost like clockwork. At first, I was scared, hiding under my blanket and hoping it would stop. But as time went on, I got used to it. I even started to find it comforting, a friendly hello from an unseen presence.

But it wasn't just me who heard the knocks. Friends who came over to play would often stop mid-sentence, their eyes wide with surprise, and ask, "Did you hear that?" My parents heard it too. They were initially sceptical, brushing it off as the wind or some other logical explanation. But after experiencing it themselves, they even called in a window repairman, thinking there might be some issue or woodworm. The repairman inspected every inch of the window but never found anything amiss.

As the years passed, other strange things began to happen. Doors would close on their own, lights would flicker, and sometimes, late at night, I'd hear soft footsteps in the hallway. But the knocking remained the most constant and unexplained mystery.

The house was eventually sold when I moved away for university. I often wonder if the new owners hear the knocks too, or if the ghost has found another way to make its presence known.

The Black Dust

Like countless families in Birmingham in the 1970s, we lived in two up, two down terraces that were built many years before and hadn't been modernised since. We didn't have much, but the house was ours, and it was home. That was until we decided to meddle with forces we didn't fully understand.

One rainy Saturday in Summer 1978, my older brother, Jim, brought home a Ouija board he'd found at a car boot sale. We were bored and naïve, not thinking about the possible consequences. We set it up in our living room and started asking questions, giggling nervously as the planchette moved across the board. Nothing really happened, and we each blamed each other for the glass moving.

The following day, we woke up to find a fine layer of black dust covering certain items in the room. It was most noticeable on the windowsills and under the pictures on the wall. We were confused, we couldn't afford coal and fire hadn't been lit since the end of Winter.

No source that could produce such soot could be found.

We cleaned it up, and hoped our parents didn't notice, but the next morning, it was back, the black dust covering our furniture and floors. It became almost a daily occurrence, a dark reminder of our foolish experiment.

An uneasy feeling fell over our home, Jim and I felt watched, a feeling that something was creeping into our everyday lives. It was as if we'd tainted our home with something evil, something that wasn't happy with our intrusion.

My Brother and I had watched horror movies and read paranormal books at the library, so we felt knowledgeable enough to cleanse the house. We said prayers, sprinkled salt, but the black dust kept returning as well as weird incidents that made our parents suspicious. We even tried to use the Ouija board again, hoping to communicate with whatever we'd invited into our home, but it was silent, the planchette no longer moving under our fingers.

It felt like we were living under a dark cloud, a constant reminder of the unseen forces we'd unknowingly invited into our home. Our once warm, if slightly run-down home, had become a place we resented and hated spending time in. I grew apart from my brother, we both spent as much time as possible out of the house, joining school clubs, karate club or messing around with mates. We both knew why the other stayed away, but too scared to ask. I don't know if anything happened to Jim, but he was never the same, sadly he passed away a few years ago and I never was able to ask him about the old house and the black dust.

The black dust, the eerie presence, the tainted atmosphere, they served as a haunting reminder of the day we brought a Ouija board into our home, forever changing our perception of the supernatural and each other sadly.

Nine Ladies Stone Circle Elemental

After the passing of my Father, I felt drawn to visit sacred sites, he was an atheist but always said we had a greater connection with the earth than any church. I used to laugh at his thoughts, but now he passed, I wanted to find this connection, and no doubt him as well.

It was a balmy summer day just a few months after Dad died when I decided to visit Nine Ladies Stone Circle in Derbyshire. He had always been drawn to such places, feeling an inexplicable connection to their history and energy.

I have never had a paranormal experience or been interested in them but as I walked among the stones, I was struck by a sudden cold spot, a chilling contrast to the warmth of the day. The stones sit in the middle of a sparse woodland on the verge of moorland, the sun shone brightly that day, but yet I was stood in the circle, cold and overcome.

This wasn't just an ordinary temperature drop. It was intense, a cold that seeped into my bones, making me shiver uncontrollably. I felt a presence, something potent and ancient. It felt elemental, a powerful entity tied to the earth and the stones.

The feeling was so strong, so overwhelming that it made me feel dizzy and queasy, I left straight away. It felt as if the elemental was warning me away, asserting its dominion over the ancient stone circle.

Ever since that day, I've been hesitant to return. The experience was too intense, too unnerving. But I've often wondered if anyone else has experienced something similar at the Nine Ladies Stone Circle. Has anyone else felt the chilling presence of the elemental?

Business Centre Ghost

I'm leasing office space in a new business centre on the outskirts of Leatherhead, Surrey. Despite its modern facade, the centre had an eerie, unsettling feel to it.

From the day we moved in, strange things began to happen. Doors would slam shut with no apparent cause. Lights would flicker, and items would inexplicably move from their places, all classic signs of poltergeist activity.

Initially, we brushed these off as electrical faults or careless mistakes. But as the incidents increased in frequency, the unease among my staff grew. It was as if the building itself was alive, watching us, playing tricks on us.

We decided to seek help and called in a well-respected spiritualist. She spent a day one weekend, in the building, exploring every nook and cranny. She concluded that the building might be haunted, not by a ghost attached to the building itself, as it was a new construction, but possibly to the land it was built on.

She suggested something terrible might have occurred on the land many years ago, a tragedy lost in the annals of history. She performed a cleansing ritual, hoping to calm the restless spirit.

Did it work? Well, the strange incidents decreased, but they never stopped completely. We still find things moved around inexplicably. Doors still close on their own, and a chill can sometimes be felt in certain parts of the building.

Considering the quiet reputation of Leatherhead, it's ironic that our business centre might be one of the most haunted places in Surrey. It's certainly made our workdays more interesting.

The Pretty Lady

I live in a cosy home in Nottingham. We have two cats, a dog, and a toddler named Lily. Our tale revolves around an ordinary corner of our living room, which became the centre of extraordinary happenings.

It began with our pets. They would stare intently at the same corner of the room, their gaze unwavering as if they were looking at something, or someone, we couldn't see. Initially, we brushed it off, attributing it to ultrasonic sounds that might be inaudible to us but caught by our pets.

Everything changed when Lily, barely two and a half years old, started joining the pets. She would sit with them, looking at the same corner, a puzzled look on her cherubic face.

One day, while playing with her toys, Lily pointed to the corner and said, "Pretty lady." We were taken aback. There was no one there. We asked Lily what she was seeing, and she replied in her innocent, toddler way, "Pretty lady with lights."

Chills ran down our spines. Our toddler was seeing something we couldn't. Lily didn't seem afraid. In fact, she seemed comforted by the 'pretty lady,' often waving at her or blowing her kisses.

We were left with more questions than answers. Who was this 'pretty lady'? Why was she in our home? And why could only our pets and toddler see her?

We called a medium, hoping to shed some light on this mystery. The medium told us that the 'pretty lady' was a benign spirit, a guardian perhaps, who meant no harm. She suggested that Lily and our pets were able to see her due to their purity and innocence.

As time went on, our interactions with the "pretty lady" became a regular part of our lives. We began to notice subtle changes around the house whenever she was present, the scent of fresh flowers would permeate the rooms, even though we had none in the house.

Lily would often engage in conversations with the "pretty lady," talking animatedly as if engaged in an invisible tea party. We would occasionally catch glimpses of Lily laughing and clapping her hands, as if responding to the "pretty lady's" playful antics. It was heart-warming to see our daughter find joy and companionship in the presence of this ethereal figure.

Friends and family would sit in the living room, their eyes fixed on the corner, hoping for a glimpse of the "pretty lady." Some claimed to feel a gentle touch on their arm or a cool breeze passing by, as if the spirit acknowledged their presence. The atmosphere in our home had an undeniable sense of serenity and calm, as if the "pretty lady" brought a peaceful energy with her.

We never felt any fear or unease in the presence of the "pretty lady," in fact it's probably one of the reasons why we continue to live here. We were grateful to have her as a comforting presence, watching over us and enriching our lives with her ethereal existence.

Telephone Call from Beyond

My name is Patricia, and I experienced something that has left me baffled and searching for answers.

My mother passed away several years ago, a devastating loss that I've tried to cope with ever since. We were very close, and I often longed for one more conversation, one more chance to hear her voice.

One rainy evening, as I was watching television, my phone rang. The caller ID displayed a number I hadn't seen in years - my mother's old telephone number. My heart skipped a beat. It was impossible. We had disconnected the line after her passing.

I answered the call, my hand trembling. The line was filled with static, and I could barely make out a faint whispering sound, but no distinct words. The call ended abruptly, leaving me staring at my phone in disbelief.

Thinking it must have been a mistake, maybe the number had been reassigned, I decided to call back. But the operator's voice informed me that the number was disconnected. I was stunned. How could a call come from a disconnected number?

I reached out to the telephone company, hoping for a logical explanation, but they were as baffled as I was. They confirmed that the number was indeed disconnected and hadn't been reassigned.

Was it a glitch in the system? Or was it something more? Was it a message from my mother from beyond the grave? I was left with more questions than answers.

To this day, I am still seeking answers, still wondering if it was a sign from my mother.

The Silent Guide

My name is Robert, and for years, I've volunteered at one of the most popular National Trust properties in the country. I'm not at liberty to disclose which one, but let's just say it's a place steeped in centuries of history and intrigue, a little clue there for you.

As part of my duties, I lead tours around the property, sharing fascinating stories about its past. Over time, I noticed peculiar happenings that couldn't be easily explained.

Footsteps echoed in the empty halls, doors creaked open on their own, and lights flickered without reason. However, the most unsettling occurrence was the spectre that made its presence known on more than one occasion.

On my evening rounds, I often saw a figure in the corner of my eye. A lady, dressed in period attire, wandering the halls. As soon as I turned to look at her, she would vanish. This figure never made a sound, never interacted, but her presence was palpable.

Visitors sometimes mentioned feeling a 'cold spot' in the grand hallway or catching a glimpse of a 'woman in a long dress' in the mirror hanging in the parlour. I kept these instances to myself, not wishing to alarm anyone.

One winter's evening, while locking up, I saw her. She stood at the top of the grand staircase, as real as any living person. Her gaze met mine, a sad smile on her face, and then, she simply faded away.

As the years went by, my fascination with the mysterious lady in period attire grew stronger. I became determined to uncover her identity and understand her connection to the historic property. I spent countless hours in the archives, pouring over dusty documents and fragile journals, searching for any mention of a woman who matched her description.

One day, while sifting through a box of old photographs, I stumbled upon a sepia-toned image that sent shivers down my spine. It was a portrait of a woman, her delicate features reminiscent of the spectre I had encountered so many times. The photograph had a caption inscribed on the back: "Eleanor Fairchild, Lady of the Manor." (Name changed at the request of the National Trust)

My heart raced with excitement as I delved deeper into the life of Eleanor Fairchild. She had lived in the property during the late 18th century, a time of opulence and grandeur. Eleanor was known for her charitable endeavours and her unwavering dedication to the local community.

However, her life had been marred by tragedy. It was said that Eleanor lost her husband and two young children within a span of a few years, plunging her into deep sorrow. She withdrew from society, becoming a recluse within the walls of the property she called home.

According to accounts from that era, Eleanor was often seen wandering the halls, dressed in black mourning attire, her eyes filled with sorrow. On some nights it was alleged that locals saw Lady Eleanor in her coach and horses, in full mourning attire thundering down the lanes close to the Manor.

Rumours circulated that she was searching for her lost children or perhaps seeking solace from her grief.

As I pieced together the fragments of Eleanor's life, the pieces of the puzzle began to align. The sightings of the lady in the long dress, the cold spots, and the sorrowful atmosphere that occasionally engulfed the property—everything pointed to Eleanor's lingering spirit.

Armed with this newfound knowledge, I shared my discoveries with the National Trust officials responsible for the property. They were intrigued by my findings and encouraged me to incorporate the story of Eleanor Fairchild into the official tours. The tale of the Lady of the Manor became a highlight of the visitors' experience, adding an extra layer of intrigue to their exploration.

Over time, as the story of Eleanor Fairchild became more widely known, other staff members and volunteers at the property began sharing their own encounters with her. They recounted seeing glimpses of her in the corner of their eyes or feeling a chilling presence when walking through certain rooms. It seemed that Eleanor's spirit was not just confined to the grand staircase but roamed throughout the property, forever tied to the place she had called home.

Rather than being frightened by her presence, the staff and volunteers developed a deep respect for Eleanor. We saw her as a guardian spirit, watching over the property and its visitors, perhaps still searching for the solace she had never found in life.

As for me, I continued leading the tours with newfound enthusiasm, sharing Eleanor's story with reverence and a touch of awe. I would often pause at the grand staircase, where I had first encountered her, and feel a connection to the past, a bridge between the living and the ethereal.

Unfortunately, around five years ago a new area manager requested that we stopped mentioning the stories of Eleanor since a distant family member had written to him and said he felt it was disrespectful. This was far from the truth, but due to the request, we only mention Eleanor if asked. I feel privileged that I have not only seen Eleanor's spirit but also unravelled her tale, sharing her story with those who visit her home.

The Old Railway Tunnel

I've got a tale to tell from my childhood, a time when a simple dare turned into a chilling encounter.

Growing up in a small Yorkshire town, my friends and I would often play near an old, disused railway tunnel. One day, egged on by each other, we decided to explore the tunnel. Armed with nothing more than our courage, we stepped into the enveloping darkness, the chill of the damp walls sending shivers down our spines.

We had barely made it a few feet in when we heard it - a cough. Not one of us, but a deep, guttural cough echoing from deeper within the tunnel. We froze, our hearts pounding. Mustering our courage, we decided to leave, vowing to return the next day, better prepared.

The following afternoon, armed with flashlights, we ventured deeper into the tunnel. The beam of our flashlights cut through the darkness, revealing the damp stone walls and a silence so profound it was almost deafening.

That's when we saw him. The beam of our flashlight fell on a figure— a man, dressed like an old navvy - a railway workman. He was as solid as any living man, then, just as suddenly as he had appeared, he faded away, leaving us in stunned silence.

We ran from the tunnel, fear lending speed to our feet. From that day onwards, we never ventured near the old railway tunnel again. The image of the old navvy, forever etched in our memories.

Years later, as adults, my friends and I would occasionally reminisce about that fateful encounter in the old railway tunnel. One evening, during one such conversation, my friend Sarah revealed something she had never mentioned before. She confided in us that her mother, Mrs. Thompson, had also experienced a chilling sighting in the vicinity of the tunnel. Sarah recounted the story with a mix of amusement and unease, aware of the strange and unnerving nature of her mother's encounter.

Sarah's mother had been a rebellious child and one autumn afternoon after the railway line had closed, she decided to explore the footpath that followed it. When she reached the tunnel, she has a mix of excitement and trepidation and cautiously stepped into the tunnel, her footsteps echoing eerily against the walls. As she ventured deeper, a sense of unease washed over her. The air felt heavy, suffused with an otherworldly energy that prickled at her senses.

Just as she was about to turn back, Mrs. Thompson heard a sound, a low moan that sent chills down her spine. She swung her flashlight around, and her breath caught in her throat. Standing a few feet away was a figure, an ethereal presence dressed in tattered clothing, resembling an old navvy from a bygone era.

With a mixture of terror and disbelief, her body reacted involuntarily, and in her distress, she had an embarrassing bodily reaction. The shock of the encounter caused her to defecate, a mortifying moment that added an unexpected layer of humiliation to an already terrifying experience.

As if sensing her vulnerability, the ghostly navvy dissipated into thin air, leaving Mrs. Thompson trembling, and shaken. She stumbled out of the tunnel, a mix of fear and embarrassment coursing through her veins. It was an encounter she would never forget, one that would become a vivid and sometimes macabre story passed down through generations.

The sighting left Mrs. Thompson with a deep-seated fear of the supernatural, and she became fervently superstitious, avoiding any mention or proximity to ghostly tales. It took her years to overcome the residual terror that clung to her from that day in the tunnel.

It also explained why Mrs Thompson was also too quickly dismissing our stories when we rushed back home to tell her of our sighting.

With Sarah's revelation, our childhood memories took on a new dimension, we couldn't believe that all this time, Sarah's mother had witnessed the Old Navvy long before we had even been born.

The Black Swan Ghost

My mother never believed in ghosts. That was until she visited The Black Swan in York, a pub with a history that stretched back centuries.

One evening, she decided to use the loo located at the top of an old wooden staircase. As she was walking up the stairs, she stopped in her tracks. She swore she saw a pair of legs ahead of her, running up the stairs. The legs appeared to be clad in pinstriped trousers. She called out, assuming it was another patron, but there was no response.

Reaching the top, she found the space empty. The sight left her puzzled, but she dismissed it as a trick of the light.

When she returned to her seat, she shared the odd incident with the landlord. His reaction was not what she expected. He went pale and told her that she might have seen the pub's famous ghost, a gentleman from the Victorian era known for his pinstriped trousers.

According to the landlord, the apparition hadn't been seen for quite some time. He was known to frequent the upper room of the pub, and many patrons had reported hearing footsteps running up the stairs, even when there was no one there.

My mother, the ever-sceptical realist, had become a witness to the pub's spectral inhabitant. The encounter didn't convert her into a believer overnight, but it gave her a story to tell, a personal encounter with the unexplained.

MJ Wayland writes, situated on Peasholme Green, the Black Swan is a site steeped in history and supernatural tales. Built originally as a private residence in 1417, the Black Swan eventually transformed into a pub in the late 18th century, maintaining much of its original structure and charm.

The pub is said to be home to several ghosts, each with its own unique story. One of the most notable apparitions is a workman sporting a bowler hat who is often seen fidgeting and tutting as if impatiently waiting for someone. Other spectral residents include a gentleman who frequents the bar, a lady who stares into the fireplace, and even the ghost of a cat that is known to perch on the end of guests' beds.

Paranormal investigators have reported experiencing cold spots, high transient EMF readings, and capturing voices, among other phenomena, during their investigations at the pub. It's no wonder then that the Black Swan Inn has been voted into the top 10 most haunted places to book a room in the UK, and the top five most haunted pubs in York.

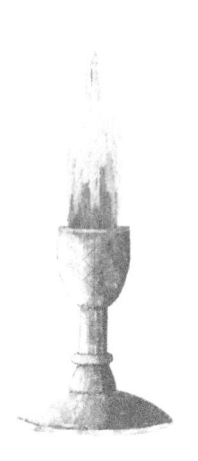

Ever-Present Companions

Max, my German Shepherd, was my sidekick for over ten years. His shiny black and tan coat, perky ears, and bright eyes were a symbol of his unwavering loyalty and affection. When he died, my home felt so much emptier. It was like his absence created a void that was so much more than physical; it tugged on my heartstrings and left me feeling alone.

In the weeks after Max's death, I started to notice some weird things. Out of nowhere, I would hear Max's body hitting the floor, the same sound he used to make when he would plop down onto our wooden floors to rest. Sometimes, I would hear scratching on the door, the same way Max would scratch when he wanted to go outside and run around the yard.

At first, I thought my mind was playing tricks on me, like my grief was causing me to hear things that weren't there. But these sounds kept happening, and they always came from the spots Max loved the most.

One night, while I was sitting on the couch in the living room, nose deep in a book, I heard the sound of Max settling down next to the fireplace, his favourite spot. I looked over, half expecting to see Max lying there, but there was nothing. Even though I couldn't see him, the room didn't feel empty. It felt warm and familiar, just like when Max was still around.

These weird experiences didn't scare me, though. They made me feel better, like Max was still with me, still watching over me like he always did. It was like his spirit was still hanging around, providing comfort in its own way.

Elaine emailed me her experiences when her dog Mitzi passed away. It had only been a few days since she had passed away, and the pain of her absence weighed heavily on my heart.

Every night since her departure, I found solace in our nightly routine. I would climb into bed, pulling the covers up to my chin, and close my eyes, desperately hoping to feel even the slightest trace of Mitzi's presence. I longed for her warm body snuggled against my legs, her gentle sighs lulling me into peaceful sleep.

As the days turned into nights, a peculiar sensation began to wash over me. It started with a gentle brush against the edge of the bed, as if a phantom tail wagged in the air. Goosebumps prickled my skin as I imagined Mitzi's spirit resting beside me. I could almost feel the weight of her paws pressing into the mattress, the slight shift of the bed indicating her familiar presence.

At first, I questioned my own sanity. Was grief clouding my judgment, creating illusions to ease my pain? But deep down, I knew in my heart that something extraordinary was happening.

One night the bedroom was filled with a profound stillness, broken only by the sound of my own breath. And then, it happened. A gentle weight settled beside me on the bed, as if my loyal companion had joined me in my solitude. The mattress sank ever so slightly, moulding to the invisible form that I could almost see in my mind's eye. It was Mitzi, of that I was certain.

I lay frozen, afraid to disturb the delicate presence beside me. The air seemed charged with love and bittersweet memories, mingling with the scent of Mitzi's fur that still lingered on her bed. It was a mixture of joy and sorrow.

With tears streaming down my face, I whispered into the silence,

"Thank you, my sweet Mitzi. I feel your presence, and it brings me comfort in this sea of grief. You may have crossed the rainbow bridge, but your spirit remains by my side, and I am eternally grateful."

Sceptics may scoff, dismissing my experiences as mere imagination, but to me, the bond between Mitzi and me is as strong as ever, in life and death.

Unwanted Gift

My name is Denise, and I've been married to Sam for twenty years. Sam always had an uncanny knack for experiencing the unexplainable. He'd often mention seeing figures that others couldn't, hearing whispers in silent rooms, and feeling presences in empty spaces. I dismissed it as Sam's active imagination until one night, everything changed.

It all started subtly. Sam began to mention the ghosts more frequently. He would see a woman in a long dress standing at the end of our garden, or a man in an old-fashioned suit staring out of the attic window. I never saw any of it, and I was more worried about Sam's mental health than any potential supernatural occurrences.

One day, to placate Sam, I invited a local medium for a consultation. The medium, a kindly older woman named Cazzie, listened carefully to Sam's experiences. After a long pause, she turned to us and said, "Sam, you have the gift. You're a natural medium. These spirits, they're attracted to your energy."

Sam looked taken aback, but I was downright sceptical. The idea of my husband being a magnet for the supernatural was absurd to me. I thanked Cazzie for her time and decided to seek a more scientific explanation for Sam's experiences.

Things escalated one night when Sam was literally thrown out of bed. I woke up to a loud thud and found Sam on the floor, shaken and scared. He insisted that an unseen force had pushed him, and there was genuine fear in his eyes. I couldn't dismiss it this time; I felt the chilling shift in the room's energy myself.

That incident marked a turning point. I could no longer ignore the fact that something beyond my understanding was happening. I was scared, not just for Sam, but also for what this meant for us.

We started seeking professional help, from psychologists to spiritual counsellors. We even had Cazzie back for a thorough cleanse of our house. But the phenomena continued, and Sam's experiences intensified.

Now, we're at a crossroads. Do we accept this 'gift' as Cazzie called it, and learn to live with it? Or do we continue to search for answers, hoping for a solution that might not exist?

If anyone out there has experienced something similar or has any advice, we're all ears. We're just trying to make sense of the senseless and find peace in our own home.

Sam wanted to tell his version of the story as well.

I'm Denise's husband, Sam, and I've been burdened with this terrifying ability. I can see the unseen, the apparitions that exist on the fringes of our reality. For years, these sightings were sporadic, manageable even. But recently, they've become more frequent, more intense, and more frightening.

The spirits I see aren't benign shadows, they're people from another era, trapped in our world. This is only my point of view, but I often see a lady dressed in Victorian attire wandering our garden, her gaze lost in the distance. In our attic, I see a man in a suit from the 1920s stares out the window, seemingly waiting for someone.

Denise, my wife, used to dismiss my experiences. I can't blame her. It's hard to believe in something you can't see or feel.

One day we asked our local medium Cazzie, and she confirmed my worst fears. She claimed I was a natural medium, a beacon for these lost souls. The news was both validating and terrifying.

That night, as Denise and I slept, I was abruptly woken by a forceful shove. I was flung from our bed, landing painfully on the hardwood floor. I looked around, expecting to see an intruder, but the room was empty. It was then that I realised, whatever had thrown me out of bed wasn't visible to the naked eye.

The incident scared Denise. I could see it in her eyes, the scepticism replaced by fear. From that point on, our lives became a whirlwind of doctors, therapists, and spiritual advisors. We were searching for answers, for a solution to a problem we barely understood.

The presence of the spirits became more oppressive. I could feel their despair, their confusion. It was as if I was living in two worlds, constantly shifting between the living and the dead. I was losing sleep, losing peace, and I feared I was losing myself.

Denise and I are thinking of moving homes. The idea is painful; after all, we'd spent years building our life in this house. But the paranormal activity is taking a toll on our lives, and we fear for our sanity.

Still, we're uncertain. Would moving solve our problem? Or would these spirits follow me, given my unwanted gift? We're desperate for answers, for some guidance.

It Followed Me Home

When I decided to visit Fountains Abbey in North Yorkshire, I was expecting a day filled with exploration and history.

Fountains Abbey, set in the picturesque Skell valley, is one of the largest and best-preserved ruined Cistercian monasteries in England. Founded in 1132, the Abbey thrived for over 400 years, until King Henry VIII's Dissolution of the Monasteries in 1539. Walking through the ruins, you can't help but feel the weight of the centuries, the monks' devotion, and the quiet despair of the place being abandoned.

I spent the day wandering through the preserved cloister, the vast refectory, and the solemn cellarium where the lay brothers slept. The delicate tracery of the chapel window, the towering arches of the nave, and the silent beauty of the monks' private chapel, all spoke of a rich, spiritual past. The silence was heavy with prayer and contemplation, the ancient stones seemed to breathe with history.

As the day was drawing to a close, I found myself in the chapter house, once the meeting place for the monks. The setting sun threw long shadows, casting an eerie glow on the ancient stones. Suddenly, I saw a figure near the archway leading to the cloister. It was a man dressed in a simple robe, his head bowed, appearing as though he was deep in prayer. I blinked, and he was gone. A shiver ran down my spine. Had I just seen a ghost?

Shaken but fascinated, I left the Abbey and returned home. That night, as I lay in bed, I heard an unsettling sound. It was like the shifting of stones, a soft, scraping sound coming from the loft. My heart pounded in my chest as I remembered the robed figure from the Abbey. Had the spirit followed me home?

The sounds persisted for a few nights, always starting around the same time, around midnight, the so-called witching hour. I considered calling someone, a medium perhaps, or a priest, but was hesitant. What if I was just imagining things?

I decided to return to the Abbey, to see if I could find any answers.

As I stood in the chapter house, where I had seen the figure, I spoke aloud, hoping the spirit would hear. I told him I meant no harm, that I respected his peace, and asked him to let me live in peace too. The Abbey was silent, the only response was the wind rustling through the ancient stones.

That night, the sounds stopped. The loft was silent, the nights peaceful. I don't know if the spirit heard my plea or if it was just my imagination running wild. But I've learned one thing, history isn't just recorded in books or etched in stone. Sometimes, it lingers in the shadows, walks in the cloister, and follows you home.

The Horfield Common Horror

Horfield Common, a quaint park on the outskirts of North Bristol, was our sanctuary. I would take Basil, my dog to wander through the manicured grass and towering trees. However, there was an area of the park that Basil hated, the area near Weston Crescent.

Every time we would approach this area, Basil would begin to act strangely. Usually docile and obedient, Basil would growl, his eyes wide with fear, his body tense. He would pull at his leash, trying to steer us away from that area. I could not understand his behaviour, but I respected it and would change our path.

This strange occurrence became a pattern. Basil's fear seemed to intensify with every passing day. I even noticed him whimpering on a few occasions. I began to wonder if he was sensing something I couldn't.

Years passed, and Basil and I continued our daily walks, always avoiding the dreaded Weston Crescent area. Basil grew old, his sprightly step slowing down, but his fear of that area never faded.

One day, while chatting with a long-time resident of the neighbourhood, I learnt something that sent chills down my spine. Many years ago, a murder had occurred near Weston Crescent. A chilling crime that had shocked the peaceful community. The area where Basil had always refused to go was the exact spot where the crime had occurred.

A sudden realisation hit me. Could Basil have been sensing the residual energy of the violent act? Could he have been reacting to the lingering paranormal energy? The idea seemed far-fetched, yet it was the only explanation that made sense.

I now look back at those walks with a sense of wonder and unease. Basil is no longer with us, but his strange behaviour near Weston Crescent will forever remain a vivid memory. Was my loyal companion more in tune with the other side than I could ever comprehend? I guess I'll never know.

Another Horfield Common Experience came to me when I asked the people of Bristol if they knew anything of its local and paranormal history. The following witnesses contact me, here is their story.

I noticed an article in the local newspaper. The article, written by MJ Wayland, a well-known paranormal researcher, detailed numerous accounts of alleged ghost sightings in and around Horfield Common. I read the article with interest, as it mentioned the area around Weston Crescent, the same area that always made me feel uneasy.

A few weeks after reading the article, I had my own experience. It was a typical evening, the sun setting, casting long shadows across the park. As I approached Weston Crescent, an uncomfortable feeling swept over me. The air seemed to grow colder, and a dense silence fell over the area.

Suddenly, out of the corner of my eye, I saw what looked like a shadowy figure, standing near the edge of the path. I turned to look directly at it, but there was nothing there. I looked around, expecting to see someone else, but I was alone.

Feeling a bit unnerved, I quickened my pace, trying to shake off the eerie feeling. But as I looked back one last time, there it was again. The shadowy figure, standing silently, watching. I could almost make out the features - a tall figure, draped in what seemed like a long coat.

I rushed home, the image of the figure seared into my memory. Over the next few days, I found myself unable to shake off the experience. I decided to write to MJ Wayland, detailing my experience. His response was as intriguing as it was chilling. He mentioned that other people had reported similar sightings, all around the same area.

Today, I still walk through Horfield Common, but I give Weston Crescent a wide berth. The memory of that shadowy figure still sends chills down my spine. Whether it was a trick of the light or something more, I'll never know.

Another witness contacted me about their father's incident that happened over fifty years ago on Horfield Common.

I grew up hearing tales of Horfield Common, the peaceful park nestled in North Bristol. My father used to work late hours, often traversing the park's paths on his way home. One area he'd always pass through was Weston Crescent, a quiet stretch of the park that always had an eerie calmness to it.

In the 1960s, something happened that forever changed my father's relationship with Horfield Common and, more specifically, with Weston Crescent.

One night, my father came home from work unusually late. His usually rosy complexion was as pale as the moonlight that filtered in through the window, and there was a wild look in his eyes that I'd never seen before. I was a young girl then, but I still remember the stark fear that etched his usually jovial features, especially after having a quick pint with his workmates.

He never spoke of what he saw that night, and we never probed. But whatever it was, it left a deep imprint on him. From that night onwards, he would take the longer route home, avoiding Weston Crescent at all costs. Whenever he had to pass the area during the day, he would walk briskly, his gaze firmly fixed ahead, never wandering towards the Crescent.

Years later, after my father had passed on, I happened across an article in the local newspaper. It was by MJ Wayland, detailing stories of ghostly apparitions in Horfield Common. My heart skipped a beat when I saw the mention of Weston Crescent.

I reached out to Mr. Wayland, sharing my father's story without revealing what he had seen, for I didn't know myself. He replied to my letter with a chilling piece of information. Apparently, several others had also reported unsettling occurrences around the same area.

The revelation sent shivers down my spine. I couldn't help but wonder what my father had seen that night that had left him so shaken. Was it one of these apparitions? Or something else entirely? I guess I'll never know.

Now, in my seventies, I often pass by Horfield Common, and each time, I can't help but glance at Weston Crescent, a silent tribute to my father and the unspeakable horror he might have faced. It's a grim reminder that sometimes, some stories are better left untold.

Tin Mine Ghost

I'm not the best at writing, but I hope you can understand my story. I'm from Cornwall, a place famous for its sandy beaches, old tin mines, and some spooky stories.

One cold night, my friends and I thought it'd be fun to check out the old, unused South Wheal Frances tin mine. We were young and brave, looking for a small adventure.

We walked far into the mine, and the only light we had come from our not-so-bright flashlights. Suddenly, my friend Billy, who's usually the joker, shouted out in surprise. He said he saw something move in the dark. We thought he was just trying to scare us. But then, I saw it too.

Out of the complete darkness, something that looked like a person appeared. It looked like a miner, wearing old-fashioned clothes, a hard hat on his head, and holding a pickaxe. He didn't move, just stood there glowing in a strange light. Seeing him made me feel really scared.

We didn't wait around to see if the ghostly miner would do anything.

We ran out of there as fast as we could, hearts racing and heads full of what we had just seen. We never went near that mine again after that.

Now, whenever I see one of those old, quiet tin mines, I always think of the ghost miner, stuck forever in the dark.

I thought you might want to hear about this. Maybe you could find out more about this ghostly miner.

As a paranormal author, stories like these sent in by witnesses are the lifeblood of my research. The account of this particular witness plunged me into a deep dive into the history of the South Wheal Frances mine in Cornwall. Known for its historical significance and the veil of mystery that surrounds it, this location is often lauded as one of the most haunted sites in the region.

The mine, which was operational in the 19th and early 20th centuries, is now abandoned, leaving only echoes of its past. Throughout its working life, it was fraught with danger, from cave-ins to hazardous working conditions. Countless miners lost their lives, leading to tales of haunting spectres, forever trapped in its depths.

One ghost story that stands out is that of a miner who met an untimely end due to a collapse. It's said that his apparition, complete with hard hat and pickaxe, can still be seen wandering the mine, eternally performing his duties from life.

Whispers of ghostly footsteps echoing through empty tunnels, flickering lights seen from the corners of one's eyes, and distant, mournful cries thought to be those of trapped miners - all these add a chilling layer to the historical tapestry of South Wheal Frances mine.

Despite its eerie reputation, the mine attracts paranormal enthusiasts and investigators, looking to document the ethereal residents of the mine or hoping to have an encounter of their own. The ghostly miner's tale, as well as many others, continues to haunt the memories and imaginations of those who visit, adding to the mystique of the South Wheal Frances mine.

Thundridge Church

This chilling tale was shared with me by an experienced paranormal investigator who has had many encounters with the inexplicable. However, one of the most remarkable experiences transpired during an investigation at Thundridge Church in Hertfordshire.

Thundridge Church, also known as St Mary's, is a 15th-century ruin surrounded by tales of ghostly sightings and chilling whispers. We'd heard stories of spectral monks, eerie apparitions, and disembodied voices. Naturally, we were intrigued.

As the twilight faded, our team set up equipment: EMF detectors, thermal cameras, and audio recorders. We hoped to capture some tangible evidence of the church's spectral inhabitants.

As the night fell, a heavy sense of anticipation enveloped us. We began our vigil, splitting into smaller groups to cover the church and the surrounding graveyard. As we settled in, the cold seemed to bite deeper. An eerie quietness fell, even the sounds of nocturnal creatures seemed muffled, distant.

My team was in the nave, the heart of the now-roofless church. We had just started an EVP session, asking questions into the silence, hoping to capture a ghostly response, when a sudden cold breeze swept through the ruined walls. The temperature dropped drastically - our breaths fogged in the icy air.

Suddenly, our EMF detector started beeping furiously. We all froze, staring at the device. The temperature continued to drop, and then we heard it - a faint, almost inaudible, sound of chanting. It was a deep, harmonious chorus, coming from nowhere and everywhere at once.

The moment was fleeting. The chanting faded, the EMF readings returned to normal, and the temperature began to rise. We were left in stunned silence, trying to make sense of the strange occurrence.

For the rest of the night, we attempted to recapture that moment, but the spectral choir remained silent. We were left with just an EVP recording, the spike in the EMF, and a chilling memory.

That night at Thundridge Church still haunts me. It was a real-life encounter with something that defied logic and understanding, a glimpse into the spectral world that exists alongside our own. Even now, the sound of the ghostly chant echoes in my mind, a ghostly melody forever etched into the history of Thundridge Church.

Another witness – but this time in the day.

My husband and I have always had a fascination with the paranormal. It was one of the things that brought us together. We often spent our weekends visiting reputedly haunted locations, hoping to catch a glimpse of the unknown.

Our journey led us to Thundridge Church, Hertfordshire one sunny afternoon. This 15th-century ruin, surrounded by nature reclaiming its place, had a reputation for being haunted. Tales of spectral monks and ethereal chanting had drawn us there.

With the sun high in the sky, the church didn't seem eerie at all. It was peaceful, almost beautiful in its decay. We wandered around the ruins, taking pictures and absorbing the atmosphere.

As we stepped into the nave, the temperature noticeably dropped. We exchanged a look; our excitement growing. It was a sunny, warm day, yet inside the church's crumbling walls, it felt like stepping into a refrigerator.

With curiosity piqued, we decided to sit and observe. The church was silent except for the distant chirping of birds and the rustle of leaves in the wind. As we sat there, the peace was suddenly disrupted by a low hum.

It was a soft, rhythmic murmur, seeming to emanate from the very stones of the church. As we listened, it slowly took shape into what sounded like a chant - a hauntingly beautiful, rhythmic cadence echoing through the nave.

We exchanged wide-eyed glances. The spectral choir we'd heard so much about was serenading us in broad daylight. The sound lasted for a few minutes before it faded away, leaving behind an intense silence.

Woodhead Pass Lights

As a female taxi driver, I've seen my fair share of odd things over the years but one night, while driving over the Woodhead Pass, I saw something that has left me questioning my scepticism about the paranormal.

It was a typical late-night shift. The radio was humming softly, and the road was almost deserted as I navigated the curving roads of the Pass. When I passed by Crowden, a small hamlet nestled in the hills, I noticed something strange out of the corner of my eye.

In the field to my right, there were small balls of light. They weren't like any lights I had seen before. They weren't the sharp, artificial lights of a flashlight or a car. They were soft, almost ethereal, and they were moving, hovering above the ground, bouncing lightly like they were weightless.

To my astonishment, they started following my taxi. They trailed behind me for about two miles, darting back and forth, seeming to mimic the movement of my taxi. As much as I tried to rationalize it, I could not explain what I was seeing.

And then, just as suddenly as they had appeared, they shot across the road right in front of my taxi, leaving a trail of light behind them. And then they vanished, disappeared into the night as if they had never been there.

I continued my drive, my heart pounding, my mind racing. I've never believed in ghosts, spirits, or anything of the sort. But that night on the Woodhead Pass, I saw something I can't explain. It's left me questioning what I thought I knew, and I can't help but wonder - what exactly did I see that night?

Another witness contacted me earlier this in January 2023.

I'm writing to you with an unusual encounter that I experienced in the Longdendale Valley last year. As an enthusiastic but new hiker, I was wild camping alone, nestled in the heart of the serene and captivating landscape with the lights of Manchester far in the distance.

As nightfall set in, I had just settled into my sleeping bag, the gentle hum of the valley's nocturnal life serving as a soft lullaby. But, as I was about to drift into sleep, an unexpected sound pierced the silence - a low buzzing noise that resembled an electrical hum from a pylon in rainy or foggy weather. It seemed to permeate the air, stirring up a sense of unease within me.

Then, out of nowhere, I spotted a faint glow. It was soft and ethereal, distinct from any natural light I've seen before. Through the tent canvas it looked as if it was a distant sky lantern or maybe an aeroplane setting off from Manchester. Then one light became two, then four and before I knew it, the tiny glowing orbs moved towards my campsite.

I slowly opened the tent door and looked into the night. There moving in an erratic pattern, flickering and dancing around my tent was these bright little balls of light. They emitted an otherworldly glow, both mesmerising and terrifying. I watched, entranced yet afraid, as these lights played their strange dance around me.

Suddenly, in a blaze of spectral light, the orbs shot up into the night sky, while others simply 'blinked out', disappearing as quickly as they had materialised, leaving behind only the silence of the valley. The hum that had accompanied their appearance had vanished, and all that was left was the sound of my own heartbeat, echoing loudly in the quiet night.

MJ Wayland writes, Crowden is in Longdendale Valley in the Peak District, famed for its high strangeness incidents that involved UFOs, strange monsters, ghosts and of course, lights.

The captivating Longdendale Lights have bewitched all who have encountered them. For over a century, these mesmerising orbs of light have defied rational explanation, evoking a sense of wonder and intrigue.

Illuminating the darkened landscape, witnesses describe these ethereal manifestations as floating spheres, radiating a kaleidoscope of vibrant hues. Locals and visitors alike have shared accounts of encountering these enigmatic lights, their presence both awe-inspiring and enigmatic.

Some believe they may be the spirits of bygone miners, forever linked to the valley they once toiled in. Others ponder natural phenomena, such as phosphorescent gases or atmospheric anomalies. Regardless of the theories, the Longdendale Lights continue to appear without explanation!

Haunting Memories of Repton School

As an old Reptonian, the memories of my time at Repton School in Derbyshire have stayed with me throughout my life. It's not just the education or the friendships I formed there that I remember; it's also the strange occurrences that took place within its ancient walls, particularly in the dormitory I was assigned in the late 1960s.

Repton School was established in the 16th century, and over its long history, it has accrued a fair share of ghostly tales. I wasn't much of a believer in the supernatural when I first arrived there, but my time in one of the oldest dormitories quickly changed that.

It began with the uneasy sensation of being watched. At night, I would often wake up with a start, feeling as if unseen eyes were fixated on me. It was an unsettling feeling that soon escalated into more tangible incidents.

One winter night, I awoke to the sound of shuffling feet. In the faint moonlight that filtered through the dormitory windows, I saw a figure - a boy about our age - walking between the beds. I assumed it was one of my dorm mates, but as I watched, the figure walked straight through the wall at the end of the room.

I blinked in disbelief, my heart pounding in my chest. I quickly turned on the bedside lamp, illuminating the room, but there was no one there - everyone was asleep in their beds.

Over the next few years, the ghostly figure made several appearances, each time walking the same path and disappearing through the wall. I wasn't the only one to witness this; several of my dorm mates also saw the figure, and our reports were eerily similar.

We eventually learnt that the wall the figure walked through used to be a door, leading to another part of the school. It was rumoured that a young pupil had died in that wing in the 1800s.

The haunted dormitory wasn't the only place that housed inexplicable phenomena. The school was steeped in ancient legends, including tales of a network of haunted tunnels and the mysterious White Lady.

These tunnels, now blocked off, were believed to have been used as escape routes during the Reformation. But their dark, dank corridors were thought to be home to more than just echoes of the past. The tunnel that ran from the school to the nearby church was especially known for its eerie occurrences.

One evening, my friends and I decided to explore the spooky tunnels. We each held a flashlight and started walking into the dim tunnel. The deeper we went, the colder it got, and we all started to feel a bit scared, like we weren't alone.

Suddenly, we heard a quiet crying sound coming from deeper in the tunnel. It scared us and made our hearts beat fast. But we decided to keep going and follow the sound. We heard the crying again, and we all stopped moving. One of my friends, Michael, said he saw a woman sitting not far from us. I couldn't see her, maybe because everyone was moving their flashlights around. But when we heard the crying again, we all ran out of the tunnel as fast as we could.

We've never forgotten about that night in the tunnel. Later, we learned that the woman Michael said he saw was a known ghost at our school. She was often heard crying in the tunnels or seen walking around the school grounds late at night. People say she used to work at the school a long time ago as a Matron and lost a student she was looking after. Now she's always looking for him.

Smugglers back from the Dead?

I'm sitting here now, trying to put into words the experience we had on our family holiday to the Isle of Wight. We'd booked this adorable cottage in Chale, just down the road from Black Gang Chine. The locals were so friendly and the cottage... well, it was like stepping back in time.

But there were some things that were off right from the start. Our dog, usually a bundle of joy, absolutely refused to go into the kitchen. He'd sit at the doorway, whining, his tail between his legs. The kitchen was the oldest part of the house, dating back to the 17th century, according to the Airbnb host. It was a bit eerie; I admit.

A few days in, my Dad woke up with these weird scratches on his back. Three long, almost deliberate lines. He tried to brush it off, said he must have scratched himself in his sleep, but we all felt a bit unsettled.

The worst part though, that was when my little brother got thrown from his bed in the middle of the night. I can still remember his screams. We all rushed into his room, found him on the floor, eyes wide with terror. He kept saying something pushed him, that he didn't just fall out of the bed. He was so shaken, we all were.

When we started putting the pieces together, everything seemed to lead back to the old smuggling days of the Isle. The locals had plenty of stories about smuggler ghosts who didn't take kindly to outsiders.

It felt like we were being watched, judged maybe. It was like they didn't want us there, in their space.

It was more than just feeling watched though, it was a feeling of unwelcome, a feeling of intrusion. It was creepy, downright terrifying. It felt like they were suspicious of us, these mainlanders in their territory.

I wrote back to the witness the following information.

The Isle of Wight boasts a rich and storied history, steeped in tales of smuggling that date back to the 17th and 18th centuries. During those times, taxation on imported goods was very high. Coupled with the Island's strategic position along busy trading routes and its rugged coastline riddled with hidden coves and caves, it created an ideal environment for a thriving illicit trade.

Many inhabitants of the Isle found themselves drawn into the smuggling trade, either as active participants or silent conspirators. It was a dangerous, yet profitable, way of life. Goods such as tea, brandy, silk, and even spices were frequently smuggled ashore under the cover of darkness, evading the watchful eyes of the customs officers.

Tales of the notorious 'Chale Gang', a group of smugglers from Wheeler family lived in the very village where you stayed and are woven into local folklore. They were known to be ruthless, not hesitating to use violence if necessary to protect their illicit cargo.

Richard Platt, Isle of Wight historian wrote about Chale and the Wheeler gang, "Chale on the south coast was the home of a notorious smuggling family called the Wheelers, who lived in Box Cottage, and Chale churchyard had a reputation for other-wordly happenings that were probably deliberate scare tactics to keep nosey locals away from stored tubs."

So interestingly the Wheeler's used the paranormal to hide their activities!

The smugglers of the Isle of Wight were savvy and daring, their audacious ventures forming an integral part of the island's history. Even today, it's not uncommon to hear stories of spectral smugglers who continue to haunt their old smuggling routes and former homes, fiercely guarding their turf from modern-day intruders. It's a chilling thought that your family's unsettling experiences could be linked to these ghostly guardians of the Isle's illicit past.

Dad was never the same.

The canals of Warwickshire are a place of serene beauty, a winding network of tranquil waterways that are perfect for a peaceful day out. This was what my family and I were expecting when we decided to hire a canal boat to celebrate my Dad's 50th birthday.

The day was a hot summer one, the sun high in the cloudless sky. We enjoyed a leisurely lunch on the boat, the gentle sway of the water relaxing us. As the afternoon wore on, we found ourselves in a particularly quiet stretch of the canal, flanked by lush green fields on either side.

Suddenly, a strange chill descended upon us, the temperature dropping noticeably despite the bright sunshine. The air grew still, the chatter of birds silenced, and an eerie quiet fell over the canal.

My mum was in the boat's kitchen when she glanced out the window and gasped. There, walking alongside our boat, were the legs of what appeared to be a farmer, decked in mud-splattered wellies and coarse, brown trousers. Intrigued, my dad stepped out onto the deck to get a better look.

He barely had time to utter a greeting to the stranger before he came sprinting back into the boat, his face pale, and his eyes wide with fear. We were all taken aback by his reaction - my dad was not a man easily scared.

"Dad, what happened?" I asked, but he just shook his head, refusing to speak of it. He was visibly shaken, a far cry from the jovial mood he'd been in just moments ago.

We continued our journey, the strange encounter hanging over us like a dark cloud. We didn't speak of it for the rest of the day, the festive atmosphere replaced with a sense of unease.

My dad never spoke of what he saw that day on the Warwickshire Canal. But whatever it was, it left a deep impression on him. As for the rest of us, we couldn't shake off the memory of the sudden chill, the eerie silence, and the disembodied legs of the phantom farmer.

Strange Stories from the Old Vic

I've been reminiscing recently and thought I'd share a story with you about my good friend who was a famous TV comedian before he retired from performing. This goes back to the 1990s when he was a regular performer at the Bristol Old Vic during the Christmas season.

Bristol Old Vic is a place steeped in history and, as many say, haunted by more than just memories. One such ghost is Sarah Macready, the former manager of the theatre, who reportedly loved the place so much that she refused to leave, even after death. You've probably heard the tales - sudden cold spots, strange noises, and even sightings of a woman in Victorian garb.

Well, during one of my friend's Christmas performances, he had his own eerie encounter. After a late-night rehearsal, he was alone in the green room, when he suddenly felt a chill, despite the heating being on full blast. He then caught a glimpse of a woman reflected in the dressing room mirror. She was dressed in Victorian attire and seemed to be watching him intently.

Startled, he turned around, but there was nobody there. The room was empty. Yet, when he looked back in the mirror, the woman was still there, standing behind him. When I asked him about his experience, he said he wasn't frightened, just... surprised. He even cracked a joke, something about "not getting a single clap, even from the resident ghost!"

This happened several times throughout his stint at the Old Vic. Each time, the woman would appear, watching him silently from the mirror, before vanishing. He was convinced that it was the ghost of Sarah Macready, keeping an eye on the performances in her beloved theatre.

I know it sounds unbelievable, but knowing my friend, I'm sure he wasn't making it up. He genuinely seemed puzzled and intrigued by the whole thing. It's one of those experiences that makes you question the line between the natural and the supernatural.

I just remembered another astonishing story about my performing friend that I believe you'll find equally intriguing, if not more so. This one is eerily linked to the legendary comedy duo Morecambe and Wise, specifically the charismatic Eric Morecambe.

As you may know my friend was a fan and friend of the famous TV double act. He often spoke fondly of the times they shared together, both on and off stage. There's one incident, however, that stands out for its uncanny nature and timing.

Just a few days before Eric Morecambe's tragic demise, he had a peculiar dream. In the dream, he met Eric in a bar that he described as "otherworldly, like heaven". Eric seemed happy and at peace in the dream, laughing and joking as usual.

He woke up from the dream feeling a strange mix of emotions - a sense of warmth from the joyful encounter with Eric, but also a hint of unease, given the heavenly backdrop of their meeting. He shrugged it off, attributing it to the usual strangeness of dreams.

But then, just a few days later, as he was driving to a performance, he heard the shocking news on the radio - Eric Morecambe had passed away. I remember him telling me how his blood ran cold at the news. The dream, which had seemed so surreal just days ago, took on a chillingly prophetic light.

He often wondered if the dream had been a premonition or a subconscious intuition of Eric's imminent departure. It was a haunting experience that left him with a profound sense of the mysteries that lie beyond our understanding. Even to this day, he speaks of that dream with a sense of wonder and sadness. Thought you'd appreciate this extraordinary piece of our friend's history. It truly makes you ponder the unknown, doesn't it?

Jacobite Spirits Still Linger?

Last Summer I set off from my home, a sense of adventure brimming within me as I journeyed towards the Scottish Highlands. My destination was Scotland, a land steeped in centuries-old history and marked by landscapes that seemed to spring out of a picture book. Drawn by tales of valiant rebels and bloody battles, I had charted out a course that took me to Glenfinnan and Culloden, two key locations in the annals of Scottish history.

My first stop was Glenfinnan, nestled between Loch Shiel and rugged mountain peaks. It was here, in this breath-taking setting, that Bonnie Prince Charlie rallied the Jacobites in 1745, igniting a spark that would blaze into a full-fledged rebellion. The Glenfinnan Monument, a tall stone obelisk topped by a statue of an anonymous highlander, rose majestically by the loch, a stark testament to the passion and turmoil of those times.

I arrived at the monument late in the afternoon, just as the sun began its descent towards the horizon, painting the sky in hues of fiery red and mellow orange. The last rays of the setting sun bounced off the waters of Loch Shiel, lending the landscape an ethereal glow. As I stood at the base of the monument, the hairs on the back of my neck prickled and I felt an uncanny chill envelop me.

This was not the coolness of a passing breeze but a coldness that seeped into my bones, seemingly out of place on such a mild summer day. It was as if an unseen shadow had passed over me, chilling me to my core. My heart skipped a beat, and I looked around in alarm, expecting to find the sun hidden behind a cloud or perhaps another visitor lurking nearby.

However, there was only emptiness, punctuated by the eerie silence of the place. A wave of melancholy suddenly swept over me, as if the monument had whispered to me tales of the Jacobites' lost cause, echoing their despair through the corridors of time.

Days later, my journey took me to Culloden, a quiet and stark moor that belied the gruesome battle that took place here in 1746, marking the tragic end of the Jacobite rebellion. Strolling among the stone markers that served as grave memorials, I arrived at the one dedicated to Clan Fraser, infamous for the high number of warriors it lost in the battle.

And there it was again. That disconcerting chill returned, creeping up my spine. This time, though, it was accompanied by a sound that sent chills down my spine - a haunting, mournful melody of bagpipes. The notes were carried on the wind, filling the desolate moor with an aura of sorrow and nostalgia. I spun around, searching for the source of the music, but there was no one in sight. No visitors, no bagpipe players, nothing. As abruptly as it had started, the music ceased, leaving only the soft whispers of the wind as they rustled through the heather.

Haunted Holiday

Me and my crew – a bunch of lads fresh out of Uni, never been much for ghost stories or any of that nonsense. We all decided to head off for a holiday in Majorca, Spain. Sun, sea, and a good bit of banter (and the rest!!!) That was the plan anyway.

We rented this old apartment, right in the heart of the city. It was one of those charming, rustic places with wooden beams, terracotta tiles, and a balcony overlooking the narrow streets. Looked great in the pictures, spacious enough for all of us. The first few days were a blast, hitting the beaches, exploring the local bars, and just soaking up the Mediterranean vibes.

But, by the fourth night, things started getting... strange.

Our mate Steve, the practical joker of the group, woke up in the middle of the night, his face pale. He said he heard someone pacing the hallway outside his room. The rhythmic tap of shoes on the stone floor. Only thing was, we were all crashed out. Hungover, probably. We laughed it off, told him he was hearing things or that it was probably some late-night reveller in the street below.

Then the next night, our stuff started disappearing. Not like, valuable stuff. But little things. Keys, wallets, sunglasses. They'd be gone, then show up in weird places. My keys, for instance, ended up in the fridge, nestled between a bottle of sangria and some leftover paella.

Who'd put keys in the fridge? Maybe I'd drunk too much? Or maybe Dave, the forgetful one, was up to his usual antics?

We thought one of us was messing around, trying to play tricks. But then, we all started waking up to these strange sounds. Like whispers. Soft, hushed voices that seemed to come from the walls. Couldn't make out what they were saying, but there was definitely something.

I remember one night, our mate Liam, the bravest of us all, woke up screaming. Said he saw a figure standing at the end of his bed, just staring at him. A silhouette, shadowy and indistinct. Now, Liam's the kind of guy who wouldn't be scared of anything, right? So, seeing him that terrified, that got to us.

We didn't want to look like a bunch of scared kids, you know? But none of us wanted to stay in that apartment. We'd go out, try to avoid coming back till we were ready to pass out. But even then, none of us could sleep properly, always feeling like we were being watched.

By the end of the trip, we were all pretty shaken. Whatever it was, it wasn't right. We couldn't explain it. We got on the plane home, and I swear, the moment we landed back in Manchester, it was like a weight had been lifted. The familiar grey skies and drizzle never felt so welcoming.

Never thought I'd be one to believe in ghosts, but after that trip? I'm not so sure. We joke about it now, call it our 'haunted holiday'. But none of us have been back to Majorca since.

And I don't think we ever will.

A Jinn or a ghost?

I'm the eldest daughter in a Syrian family who found refuge in the bustling heart of London. We were offered a compact maisonette, a little refuge nestled above a quaint shop on a busy street. It was our sanctuary in this unfamiliar world. Yet, there was something about the place that felt "off".

The shop below us, which stood vacant and silent at night, seemed to harbour an unsettling energy. Late-night bangs, unexplained clatters, and the sound of unmistakable footsteps would often echo through the quiet. The shop was always securely locked, and the alarm system remained undisturbed. It was baffling, and unsettling.

What was really disturbing was the terrible smell that would rise from the shop around 3 am. It was such a bad smell that it made us feel sick. It was a smell we couldn't identify, and it was very disgusting. Then, as quickly as it came, it would go away, leaving us wide awake and feeling really uncomfortable.

I come from a culture rich in folklore and superstition. We believe in the Jinn, supernatural entities that exist alongside us. I had always dismissed these stories as mere fables, until one unforgettable night.

The footsteps came again, but this time, they were not just below us, but in our living room. I crept out of my room, a ball of anxiety. The living room was empty, but the air was dense with something unseen.

I flicked the light switch. Nothing. The bulb had mysteriously gone out. The room was bathed in an ethereal glow from the streetlights outside. And then, a sudden rush of cold air swept past me, like a person briskly walking by.

I was suddenly aware that we were sharing our space with an unseen tenant. It wasn't threatening or harmful, but it was a persistent, unnerving presence that turned our daily life upside down. The odd occurrences became our strange new routine.

I often found myself wondering if this was a Jinn, an entity from the stories of my childhood. Was it attached to the shop, or did it come with the land? Were we disturbing it or was it merely making its presence known?

We've since moved away, and I often find myself thinking about our time in that maisonette. I wonder if the new occupants experience the same phenomena or if the spectral footsteps have finally found their peace. I don't know if I'll ever get the answers, but the experience has left me with a deep respect for the stories of my heritage.

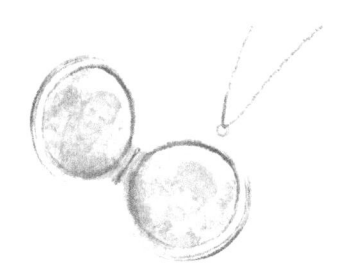

The Curse

I'm a woman from the small town of Evesham, and for a time, I was convinced I had been cursed. It all started when I crossed paths with this woman, known locally as a medium. Or a witch, depending on who you ask.

She had a shop in town, one of those 'mystic' places, filled with crystals, tarot cards, that sort of thing. I'd gone in, just out of curiosity. She offered to read my palm. I agreed, thinking it was all a bit of fun.

She told me some general stuff, then, all of a sudden, her expression changed. She said I had a dark shadow around me, a curse. Now, I didn't really believe in that stuff, but the way she said it, with such conviction, it stuck with me.

Not long after that, strange things started happening in my house. I'd hear these eerie growls, like some sort of animal. There'd be unexplained knocks and bangs. Things would move or disappear, then reappear in odd places. And the stones, they were the worst.

They'd just come from nowhere, hitting walls, windows.
I was terrified. I thought I was cursed, that the medium had done something to me. I lived in fear for weeks. I couldn't sleep, I couldn't eat. I was a wreck.

Finally, in desperation, I went to see another spiritualist. She was known for her honesty and had a good reputation. I told her everything, about the medium, the curse, the strange happenings.

She listened patiently, then told me something I didn't expect. She said that the medium in town was known for being a fake, for scaring people into buying her 'protection' charms. The 'curse' was likely just a ploy to get me to spend money.

As for the strange happenings, she suggested it could be my own fear manifesting. My mind was so focused on the idea of being cursed, it was creating these experiences. She advised me to try and let go of my fear, to ignore the strange happenings.

And you know what? It worked. As I started to dismiss the idea of the curse, the strange occurrences stopped. The growls, the knocking, the stones, it all just... stopped.

I don't know if it was all in my head or if that medium had somehow influenced it all. But I do know that I'm no longer afraid. I'm no longer living under the shadow of a 'curse'. That, in itself, is a victory.

Westbury Swimming Pool

I've always loved swimming. It's been my go-to activity for as long as I can remember, so naturally, when I moved to Westbury, Somerset, finding the local swimming pool was top of my list.

Perched on a charming street is the Westbury Swimming Pool. An imposing structure built in the 1800s, it boasted an architectural grandeur that was tinged with a sense of history. The cobblestone exterior and archaic design infused it with a peculiar allure, but it was the whispered tales of its supposed haunting that truly ignited my curiosity. Despite these spine-tingling rumours, I shrugged off the local folklore as harmless superstition.

I started going there daily, early in the morning. It was peaceful, just me and the water. But then, strange things started happening.

One morning, as I was doing my laps, I saw a shadowy figure on the poolside. It was the figure of a man, standing at the edge of the pool, watching me. I stopped, blinked, and it was gone. I shrugged it off as a trick of the light.

Another day, I heard a child's laughter echoing through the hall. I was alone, the laughter had no source. It was eerie, and it sent chills down my spine. The lifeguard assured me it was probably just the acoustics playing tricks.

But the most terrifying experience happened one winter morning. I was alone in the pool, gliding through the water, when suddenly, I felt a tug at my leg. It was strong enough to halt my movement. I panicked, thinking it was a cramp, but there was no pain, just this undeniable pressure around my ankle. I looked down into the water, but there was nothing, no one.

Adrenaline surging through my veins, I hauled myself out of the pool, my heart pounding against my ribs. I stumbled towards the changing room, my mind a whirlwind of confusion and fear. The staff, upon hearing my story, exchanged knowing glances. It was then that they disclosed the chilling tale of a swimmer who had drowned in the pool decades ago. Since then, swimmers have reported similar experiences, lending credence to my experience.

Who was Bloody Mary?

Back in the 80s, in Coventry, there stood a derelict Victorian house at the end of our road. We called it the 'Murder House', the kind of name that only a group of teenagers with overactive imaginations could come up with. With its crumbling facade and broken windows, it was the perfect setting for our little ghost-hunting escapades.

The house, probably more a victim of neglect than anything else, had an air of mystery to it. We didn't know if any murders had actually happened there, but that didn't stop the rumours. It was said to be haunted, but we were young and foolish, not afraid to poke the unknown.

One day, we gathered our courage and decided to break in. The interior was as eerie as the exterior - dust-covered furniture, peeling wallpaper and weird markings on the walls. We couldn't make head nor tail of these strange symbols, but it added to the aura of the place.

We decided to play a game - 'Bloody Mary', a silly game we'd heard about where you call upon a ghost to appear. We gathered in a circle, our faces alight with anticipation, and started chanting. At first, it was all laughs and jitters. But then, the atmosphere changed. It became cold, unnaturally cold. There were strange noises, a kind of low hum, almost like a whisper.

After a while, we stopped joking around. One by one, we started to see things - fleeting shadows, odd shapes, strange movements in the corner of our eyes. We were terrified, but none of us wanted to admit it, none of us wanted to be the first to run.

One evening, we decided to explore the cellar. It was damp and musty, filled with old boxes and broken furniture. As we descended the creaky stairs, our friend, let's call him John, suddenly froze. He pointed towards a corner of the room, his face pale as a sheet. He said he saw a figure, a dark shadowy figure, looming there. We couldn't see anything, but John was convinced. He ran out of there and never came back with us to the 'Murder House' again.

Even now, years later, he refuses to talk about what he saw that day in the cellar. The rest of us eventually moved on, leaving the 'Murder House' and its stories behind.

I also received another encounter with 'Bloody Mary' but this time in Glasgow.

Back in the 90s, I lived in one of the old tenement buildings in Glasgow. It was a sturdy, old-fashioned block with a labyrinth of rooms, each bearing the marks of the countless people who had lived there before us. It was the kind of place where stories clung to the walls like damp, breeding both warmth and unease in equal measure.

I was in my late teens then and shared the flat with a few mates. One of them, Robbie, was a prankster who loved a good scare. He was the one who introduced us to the 'Bloody Mary' game. The idea was simple: say her name three times in front of a mirror, and she would appear. It was a silly game, something we did for a laugh after a few pints.

One cold night, we'd all gathered in the bathroom, a dingy place with an old, warped mirror. We turned off the lights and lit a single candle. Robbie was in the lead, his face illuminated by the flickering candlelight. He started to chant "Bloody Mary" in a low voice. We joined in, our voices echoing in the small room. One... two... three...

Nothing happened. We laughed it off, calling Robbie an idiot and teasing him about his tall tales. But something in the room had shifted. The air was colder, and there was a strange silence, as if the building itself was holding its breath.

Later that night, I woke up to a strange sound. It was a low, scraping sound, like something being dragged across the floor. I assumed it was Robbie, trying to scare us. I decided to catch him red-handed and tiptoed across the flat to his room. I pushed the door open, ready to tell him off, but stopped in my tracks.

Robbie was in bed, fast asleep. But the room wasn't empty. In the dim light, I could see a figure standing by the old mirror. It was a woman.

She was pale, almost transparent, her face obscured by her long, dark hair. She turned and looked at me, and my blood ran cold. It was like looking into an abyss. I slammed the door shut and ran back to my room.

The next day, I told the others about what I saw. They laughed it off, said I'd had a nightmare. Robbie looked pale, but he laughed the loudest. I knew they didn't believe me, but something had changed. We stopped playing games after that, and Robbie stopped telling ghost stories.

Marcus dropped me an email in 2020 at the height of the pandemic.

I'm writing to you today because of a recent and frankly, unnerving experience that's left me quite unsure and anxious. I'm a long-time follower of your work, and I believe you might be the only one who could provide some clarity on what's been happening.

A few nights ago, my friends and I were reminiscing about childhood games, and we ended up talking about "Bloody Mary". We laughed at the memories and how we used to frighten each other with stories of her appearing in the mirror. In the spirit of nostalgia, we decided to play the game, not truly expecting anything to happen.

We gathered in my bathroom, turned off the lights, lit a candle, and chanted "Bloody Mary" three times. All of us were giggling nervously, but nothing happened. We turned the lights back on, had a laugh about it, and called it a night.

However, since then, things have been strange. I've started noticing a subtle coldness in my apartment, and I often feel like I'm not alone. I've also begun to see fleeting movements in the corners of my eyes, but when I turn to look, there's nothing there.

The most disturbing thing happened last night. I woke up in the middle of the night to a low whispering sound. It was faint but insistent. I followed the sound to the bathroom. The door was slightly ajar, and a cold draught was coming from inside. The whispering seemed to be emanating from the mirror. I turned on the light, but there was nothing unusual, and the sound stopped.

I know this might sound crazy, but I can't shake off the feeling that these occurrences are related to that night we played "Bloody Mary". I am not someone who usually believes in the supernatural, but the change in my home's atmosphere and my own growing unease are hard to ignore.

Grandad's Promise: An Unseen, Unbreakable Bond

From a very young age, I was fascinated by everything that seemed to defy the bounds of our known reality, particularly the concept of life after death. My grandad, a robust and lively character, was my partner in these deep, philosophical discussions. His wisdom, coupled with a playful sense of humour, made every conversation a memorable one.

One day, while sitting in his garden surrounded by roses in full bloom, he turned to me, his eyes twinkling with a mix of mischief and solemnity. "You know, love," he said, "When I pass on to the other side, I'll make sure to drop you a line. Just so you know I'm still around, watching over you."

I laughed it off then, a young girl who saw death as a distant, unapproachable phenomenon, something that couldn't possibly touch someone I loved. Yet, the promise stuck with me, echoing in the back of my mind over the years.

Fast forward to the day my grandad peacefully passed away. He left an indelible void in my life that seemed impossible to fill. I mourned his loss deeply, yet I held onto the promise he made me years ago. I yearned for a sign, any sign, that would tell me he was still around, still watching over me.

In the weeks following his funeral, I started noticing strange, yet comforting occurrences. It began with a whiff of his distinct pipe tobacco smell that would often waft into my room unexpectedly, a scent that had been absent from our lives since his passing. Then there was the familiar, melodious tune of his favourite song that would inexplicably play on my radio, even when I was sure I had switched it off.

Perhaps the most remarkable incident happened one calm evening when I was feeling particularly low. I sat by myself in the garden, the same garden where we had had countless conversations. As I gazed at the rose bushes, a soft breeze started to blow, and a single rose petal floated down and landed gently on my lap. I felt an overwhelming sense of peace and warmth, as though someone had wrapped me in a comforting hug.

Suddenly, I noticed a robin, a bird my grandad often said was a visitor from heaven, perched on the garden fence. It looked at me with an uncanny intensity before chirping a cheerful tune and flying away. I couldn't help but smile, feeling an overwhelming sensation that my grandad was right there with me. I've heard that some people think Robins are a sign from loved ones, while sceptics might chalk these incidents up to mere coincidence or the workings of a grief-stricken mind seeking comfort. But I choose to believe otherwise. I choose to believe in my grandad's promise.

The Thing

After an experience last night I am absolutely terrified and don't know what to do or what this "Thing" wants with me. Excuse me if some of the experiences I mention here aren't particularly paranormal, but I just really need to get this off my chest.

The first experience I remember must have been when I was about ten. I was woken up at night by a strange voice whispering my name and telling me to get out of bed. I did and stopped outside my parent's door. Then the voice spoke to me again and whispered to me to get back into bed. I did so, and that was that.

The second experience I recall was one of the ones that terrify me the most and happened a year or so after the last one. I remember I was in my room getting something, I turned around to walk out my door and saw a tall black figure flash past me. This was definitely in the shape of something humanoid, and I know what I saw. I may be wrong in this but during the next few months afterwards, I think I may have seen a black figure crouched against my ceiling twice. I may be wrong in this, but I saw the entity the first time.

Now I'm older my experiences happen randomly when it is very early in the morning (1 am to 3 am) I can hear someone downstairs, but the doors are locked, and everyone is asleep. It is always only me awake when this happens. I hear the doors banging, then someone walking upstairs. For years I could only ever hear doors creaking after that, but lately, the entity has taken to scratching against my door, knocking, and making thudding noises. It's only been the past few months that this has been happening, and I've been having a rough time of it lately, so this is the perfect end to a day!

Now the scary part. I understand if you guys don't believe me, but I'm not making it up. At night after the door banging etc. I always feel a presence at the side of my bed, always at my back. After this, I usually get a feeling of great dizziness and a feeling of being "out of it". I am convinced that this is the presence of something trying to get into my head.

I can usually fight it off, but sometimes I just fall asleep during this.

Last night was the first time I was "spoken to" since I was a kid. I got the usual head rush feeling, fought it off and then just as I was about to fall asleep, I heard a young man's voice say very clearly in my head: "Hi." I froze after this and tried to ignore it. Just as I was about to nod off again, I heard him say "you."

It sounded to me when this happened that he was mocking me, toying with me. After this, I tried to shut him out and just as I fell asleep, I got this horrible feeling that he was very annoyed with my reaction and when I woke, I felt very strongly that I had had a rough night but could remember nothing.

Don't look into the corner

My Hell in a Haunted House

It was around August in 2007, and my mom and I just bought a beautiful, two-bedroom house that had been around since the late 1800's, she insisted on moving in, but something about the house just put a shiver down my spine.

I remember the day she showed me the house, yes, it was very beautiful, it was white, with a red door, and blue shutters. As soon as I stepped on the lawn, my conscious was telling me to turn back.

So, I just stayed still, not moving and my mom said, "Honey, come on!" But still yet I didn't move, she then came up to me and shook my shoulder a little and I just fell to the ground, then my mom kneeled and asked me if I was alright, I nodded my head yes, and told her that I wasn't feeling too hot, so we just went home. I didn't even step into the house, and I knew that it was evil.

I tried telling my mom about my feelings toward the house, but her heart was set on it, I kept on telling her, not to, and not to, but she just ignored me and told me I was just being silly, and letting my imagination get to me.

She finally bought the house, and my heart just sank. It was moving day, and the ride to the house only took a good thirty minutes. As soon as we parked in the driveway, I felt that feeling in my stomach, that feeling you get before you're about to ride a rollercoaster, but instead of the excitement part, I felt the fear.

My mom walked to the front door, the key in her hands. She just couldn't wait to get in the house. We reached the door, and she pulled her hand out, the key going in the lock, then she thrust herself toward the door, but just ended up, running into it, she said, "humph, that's funny?" I just ignored her and then suddenly the door creaked open by itself. My mom's eyes got a little big, then she shook her head lightly and said, "Just the wind."

I remember walking in and feeling the cold breeze from inside the house hit my face. My mom shivered and said something about how cold it was, and I just stood there, my bags cringed in my hands.

She then walked to a hallway near the right of us, where a bathroom lay on one side, and my room lay on the other. She grabbed the doorknob and opened the door. I followed quickly not wanting to be in one room alone. She looked around the room, me now in the doorway, it was even colder in this room. She smiled and said, "Oh, It's cute! Perfect for friends and hanging out!" I sighed and thought I said something like, "if I make any friends," or something like that. She looked at me, and gave me her, Kit, just try and get used to it, look. I just looked away, and she closed the door, leaving me all alone, in that cold room that gave me nightmares for months.

The months flew by, and I wasn't making any friends. Schoolwork was getting unfinished, and I began to get stuck in the same, old rut. I remember crying almost every night. It was like hell for me; every night lying too my mom and telling her things at school were great and hiding detention slips. I had only lived in the house for a month or so and already felt depressed. I kept on complaining to my mom of what the house was doing, but she just normally tuned me out, not seeing any of the changes. I just felt like there was nothing I could do.

I remember this night vividly, I was sitting in my room, listening to music, and then I heard a slight scratch from somewhere. I looked around the room, and just continued what I was doing, and then I heard it again. So, I just got up and turned my music even up even louder. I sat down on my bed and out of nowhere, my stereo, pushed to the side of my dresser and fell to the floor all by itself. I screamed and called for my mom, but when she tried to open the door, it became stuck, and there was no way for her to get in.

She started yelling about something, but I couldn't hear her, I was too busy screaming and crying. It was like the devil himself was doing this just to amuse himself. Then the door flung open, and my mom came in looking at me with wide eyes. I was on the floor, my back against the side of my bed, crying in my arms. She just held me, and I kept on repeating, "We have to get out of this house!" over and over again. She just kept me in her arms and told me that it was alright, her eyes then narrowed toward my stereo, that was smashed on the ground, then she screamed, "What the hell happened here?" I just lay there on the floor not moving and then she just came up to me and we sat there for about an hour, sitting in the cold room.

Later, that night I was about to take a shower when I saw a red mark, near the side of my arm. I turned around and looked at my back, where scratches took over, there were six or seven big scratches that looked new, fresh. I then called for my mom, and she came in the bathroom, one of her hands covering part on her mouth, she then told me to get dressed and grab my stuff. I did as I was told and packed up my things quickly, only grabbing a few things. She then opened the front door, and we left the house.

We stayed with my aunt for the rest of the week, and left the house, which was fine by me, but from this day, whenever I think about the house it sends shivers down my spine! I never want to set foot, in that house again.

A few months after we moved out, we learned that there was a family of devil worshipers that lived there years before us. There was a little girl that had come up to the house one day, asking providence for her church and the family went mad and hung the little girl in their living room, putting candles around her hanging corpse. The family then left the country after that. I find this story, very interesting, and I wonder if it was the little girl's spirit haunting me, through those past months.

Derry's Phantom Field: A Ghostly Encounter

Just behind my house, there used to be an old, dilapidated construction site, a place that lay forgotten and shrouded in mystery. The site, home to a decaying barn house and a vast open field, was the stuff of local legends and ghost stories that had been passed down through generations. It had always intrigued me, and one day, my curiosity got the better of me. Accompanied by a friend, I decided to explore the site.

As we ventured into the unkempt field, a sudden movement caught our attention. An enormous, black figure sprang from the undergrowth, dashing across the field merely feet away from where we were standing. It was canine-like, resembling a wolf, but I knew for a fact there were no wolves in Derry. The sight of the beast sent a chill down my spine, but the unfolding events were about to turn more sinister.

Lifting our gaze to the barn house, we spotted a figure standing on the edge of the field. Cloaked in white, it was an old woman. Her appearance instantly reminded us of the dreadful stories tied to the house. Stories of a horrific fire that had engulfed the house 60 years ago, claiming the life of a two-year-old girl.

Our hearts pounded as the woman started to approach us. We were trespassing, and we assumed she would reprimand us for our audacity. But as we prepared to retreat, the black figure re-emerged, growling menacingly. Fuelled by pure terror, we sprinted back towards the safety of our home.

As we neared the edge of the field, I dared to look back one last time. The sight that met my eyes still haunts me to this day. The woman, together with the black beast, stood at the top of the field, their eyes locked on us, seemingly waiting for our return.

After that day, I swore never to step foot in that field again.

A Life of Experiences

I will start out by saying, as a child, I grew up in an old bed and breakfast, which my grandmother owned. There were strange occurrences that were felt by all members of the family. For my own personal experiences there, I saw lights from the downstairs sitting room, heard voices and footsteps, and even witnessed a small, glass object as it was lifted physically (and by unseen hands) from the mantle (might I mention, that the mantle sat over a then-boarded-up fireplace).

At 16, I moved in with a friend's family due to issues with my own family. I had visited her home many, many times before, and had gotten strange "vibes" whilst there. One evening, when we were about 14, she and I were having a phone conversation at night, when she screamed as if she had been stabbed. After a moment of listening to her frantic breathing, I asked her what was wrong.

"I just saw a head outside of my window . . ."

I didn't know what to think for a moment. Meanwhile, she took her cordless phone around the house, wanting me to listen and calm her down as she looked for whoever might be outside. No one was there. When she told her mother about the incident, she offered, "Maybe it was an owl."

However, Kat (my friend) can recall to this day seeing a black figure looking in, with head and shoulders as a visible outline to its faceless form. From then on, she kept her blinds closed.

When I moved in, things stayed fairly usual. Nothing of huge import happened for many years, actually; but when Kat's mom moved out with her husband, we were charged with the house.

As cheesy as it sounds, things got very intense on Halloween of 2008, which I believe was a Friday. I was off work, Kat didn't have classes, and her boyfriend, Jordan was not working.

Now, it is of note that we were doing nothing of any merit. I believe I had just gotten up (as it was around 10 am) and Kat was still asleep. Jordan was playing his DS on the couch. We both heard, at the same time, very loud banging and sliding noises coming from the half-bath, yet again. The half-bath was in the hall just outside of my bedroom.

This experience, I will never forget.

While I did not see anyone's hands on the drawers of the bathroom cabinet, here they were opening and closing, as if someone were looking, very hastily, for something inside of them. It only lasted for a few seconds after I had witnessed it. After I had stood, dumbfounded for a moment, I rushed into the living room and got Jordan, who was looking into the hall with a stunned expression.

That night, we invited a few other friends who were also into these things. We sat down, casually, in the living room and actually, "asked" the ghost to leave. Well, we didn't flat out ask, we asked questions, to which we got further EVPs. Such as, "What are you looking for." To which we got a reply "home".

After we had asked the ghost to either be polite, or leave, things did indeed calm down. We made it clear that we were not afraid, but confused, and that it was welcome, as long as it respected us as we did it.

Nothing ever really stopped. People would still hear the female voices in the stairs and living room (which we did catch on recorders) and sometimes, guests would 'feel' someone watching them at night.

This house was built in 1998 but was placed over the foundation of an old farmhouse which had burned down many, many years ago. The land sits on a lovely, pristine 4 acres, and is probably still occupied by special guests. I have since moved, so I do not know the state of house, as Kat's brother oversees its upkeep now. Whatever is there is not intent on hurting anyone and seems quite happy that we accepted it as just another tenant.

Haunted Caravan

I don't know much about ghosts and all that stuff but I'm pretty sure my husband renovated a haunted caravan. Sounds weird I know, but nothing else can explain it.

My hubby Tony started his own business after he retired, buying, renovating, refurbishing, and selling caravans and camper trailers. His specialty was old retro vans and people sought him out for his expertise and attention to detail.

A few years back a couple in their early 40's came in with a tired, rundown old caravan dating back to the 70's. It was a big old beauty, but it was in very bad condition. Tony got to work on it nonetheless, optimistic about its eventual restoration.

Working in the yard one day I could hear Tony calling my name from his workshop. I made my way into the shed wondering what all the fuss was about. I couldn't see Tony anywhere, so I called his name loudly. His head popped out the door of the old van with a perplexed look on his face.

"Did you just call me darl?" Tony asked me.

"Yes ... I called you because you called me ... didn't you?" I replied.

Tony then emerged from the van looking more confused. "No, I didn't ... you were calling me."

I shook my head in disagreement.

"You called me first though, didn't you?" he asked me.

Then it was my turn to be confused. Tony went on to explain that while he'd been working on the van, he'd heard me calling him. He said it sounded as though I was right behind him in the van, but when he turned around, I wasn't there, so he went back to his work. A couple of moments later he said he'd heard me call his name again, then again. That was when he'd called out to me.

Leaving us both a little baffled, we both went off to do our respective chores ... Tony back to his van and me back to the weeding in the garden.

Later that night Tony brought up the strange experience again, but the more we discussed it, the more confused we became.

The following morning, I headed into town and didn't return until early evening. Tony had closed his workshop (strange within itself) and was waiting for me in the kitchen upon my return. He looked more than just a little rattled.

"You were calling me again today," he stated before I'd even had a chance to put my handbag down. He continued, "I kept feeling like someone was watching me all day. Every time I went near the old van, I kept getting the feeling that I wasn't alone. And I'd get myself a tool to do something, but the moment I put it down it was moved or disappeared completely. I found my screwdriver up on one of the cabinets and I know I never put it there. Took me half an hour to find it."

I certainly couldn't imagine what was going on, but Tony wasn't one to make up stories.

A week or so later the owners of the van rang to see how the renovations were progressing. Tony asked them what they knew of the history of the van, and they told him that they'd bought it through a friend, so would see what they could find out.

Tony worked on the van diligently and did a splendid job of restoring it as well as installing some modern conveniences as per the owner's requirements. Each night though, after spending time working on the van, Tony would tell me about the constant feeling of being watched, hearing his name amongst other words and voices, his tools continued to vanish and turn up in odd places and it was always cold inside the caravan.

The caravan was near completion, and I was curious to take a look for myself. Tony was busy fitting new lights to the outside of the van so I took myself inside and sat on the newly refurbished couch.

I can't really explain what I felt or why, but within a few moments I felt a cold chill run right through me and I shivered involuntarily. I also got the feeling that someone was watching me from the moment I stepped inside. As much as I was determined to stick it out, I just felt so uncomfortable that I was forced out of the van. All I really know is that there was something strange about that old caravan and both Tony and I were glad to see it finally finished and out of the workshop.

When the owners arrived to pick it up, they were over the Moon about the job Tony had done on their own van ... but hadn't been able to find out the origins of the van or any information about its history. I don't think I really want to know anyway. I'm just pleased nothing like that has happened to us since.

Burning Man of RAF Woodbridge

In the year 1984, I found myself stationed at the twin bases of RAF Woodbridge and RAF Bentwaters, nestled in the English county of Suffolk. As a Sergeant, I was tasked with overseeing the Security Police flight that predominantly worked the midnight shift. Upon my arrival, I was acquainted with local information, guidelines, and various tales circulating the base, one of which caught my interest.

I was informed about an unfortunate German pilot from the World War II era, who met a fiery end at RAF Woodbridge, a designated "crash" base during the war. It was recounted how, after crashing his plane, the German pilot managed to escape the wreck, only to find himself swallowed by the flames that had engulfed his aircraft.

Responding emergency crews could only watch as the burning pilot ran around the east end of the runway, in a futile attempt to put out the flames. He ultimately fell dead near the East Gate, after leaving a set of handprints, seared onto the hood of a nearby staff car. Despite the spine-chilling tale, I dismissed it as base folklore and carried on with my duties.

However, just a few weeks later, I was destined for an encounter that would profoundly shake my beliefs in the supernatural. During one of my midnight shifts, after ensuring all my personnel were stationed at their respective posts, I proceeded to perform routine checks.

After checking on the personnel at the Main Gate and the roving patrols, I decided to visit Airman Myles at the East Gate. He seemed unusually anxious that night, mentioning strange sightings at the far end of the East Gate. I reassured him, attributing his experiences to illusions created by shifting light. I volunteered to personally investigate the area, a promise which seemed to calm him until the heavy gate unexpectedly closed on its own.

The loud, echoing clang of the gate made me jump. I exited my patrol car, pistol in hand, and thoroughly examined the surrounding area within a 100-metre radius. Despite finding no evidence of intrusion, a strong intuition told me that something was amiss. I tried to reassure Airman Myles once again, but his resolve to leave his post was unshaken. Not even the prospect of military disciplinary action seemed to deter him.

I then reported the situation to Flight Officer Lt. Freedman, explaining Airman Myles's behaviour and my own experiences. I suggested temporarily closing the gate while the area was thoroughly searched with a canine unit. The Lieutenant agreed, and as we proceeded to close the gate, we noticed a flickering light growing in intensity nearby.

The air around us seemed to charge electrically, sending the hairs on the back of my neck standing on end. I instructed Airman Myles to secure the gate while I conducted another sweep on foot. As I began to cross the road towards the blast wall, I was hit by a sudden wave of intense heat.

Airman Myles uttered in disbelief, "Oh My God, what the hell is that?" I turned to see a horrifying sight: a flaming figure, seemingly human, moving towards us. It approached our patrol car and leaned on the hood before disappearing into thin air.

Panicked, I ordered Myles to get in the car and we sped away from the scene. Upon reaching the Main Base, under the yellow glow of the parking lot lights, we noticed something astonishing. A pair of handprints were scorched into the hood of our vehicle, a chilling reminder of our encounter with the apparition.

From that night onward, if any of my personnel expressed discomfort about manning the East Gate, I didn't hesitate to close it until our spectral visitor had made his evening stroll. We'd then reopen the gate, relieved that all he seemed interested in doing was leaving behind his mark, a set of fiery handprints.

A change was noticeable in our routines following that encounter. Night shifts, once mundane and monotonous, were now filled with a sense of unease. The ethereal presence seemed to have changed the atmosphere of the entire base, making it heavy with the echoes of a past life cut short. Even the most sceptical among us became more cautious, their disbelief waning in the face of the inexplicable.

The tale of our encounter with the spectre, whom we dubbed 'East End Charlie', spread around the base, reigniting interest in the old war stories. The scepticism I initially had towards these local tales had transformed into a newfound respect. The East Gate, now infamous for its spectral resident, was treated with a combination of fear and reverence.

On quiet nights, when the base was wrapped in a blanket of stillness and the only sound was the distant hoot of an owl, it was as if time stood still. Each creak of a gate or whisper of the wind seemed to carry an eerie undertone. It was on these nights, when even the hardiest of soldiers felt a tinge of fear, that we knew we weren't alone.

4:00pm

My Aunt Barbara had a rather unsightly vintage clock that occupied a central position on the mantel above the old fireplace in her living room.

I'd always joked with her about how ugly it was, and she'd rib me in return, promising that she'd leave it to me in her will. I laughed it off, never suspecting she was serious.

As I was touring Europe, with a brief stop in London, an email from my mother delivered the unfortunate news that my beloved aunt had passed away in her sleep. Her funeral was scheduled for the following Wednesday at 4:00 PM, prompting me to arrange my return to Australia to align with the event. My flight was set to leave Heathrow at 4:00 PM the next day.

I felt a mix of sorrow and relief. Sadness at losing Aunt Barbara, and relief that she no longer had to endure the pain she'd been suffering for some time.

The funeral was an unanticipated spectacle, full of laughter amidst the tears, as we reminisced about Aunt Barbara's lively exploits and eccentricities, just the way she would've wanted.

In the days that followed her funeral, we gathered at Aunt Barbara's house to sift through her possessions. True to her meticulous nature, she had labelled each of her belongings, signifying the recipient in her will.

As it so happened, the much-maligned vintage clock was now mine. As I loaded the clock into my car, it chimed four times, announcing the hour. Aunt Barbara had always been adamant about keeping the time exact.

Once home, I positioned the clock on a coffee table in my living room. I was tempted to stash it out of sight or even out of my house altogether. However, out of affection and respect for Aunt Barbara, I chose to display it.

The clock remained silent until 4:00 AM. Its resonant chimes woke me up, making me wonder why it only chimed at 4:00 PM and 4:00 AM, but no other times. I shrugged it off and fell back asleep.

Two weeks after Aunt Barbara's funeral, my mother visited with a collection of old photos and trinkets belonging to Aunt Barbara. As we caught up over a leisurely lunch, the vintage clock chimed four times at precisely 4:00 PM.

My mother and I shared a laugh over the clock's questionable beauty and Aunt Barbara's vow to bequeath it to me. When I mentioned its peculiar habit of chiming only at four, my mother revealed a surprising fact. The number four had been Aunt Barbara's lucky number. She was born at 4:00 PM on April 4th, got married at the same time, and took her afternoon naps at 4:00 PM. Furthermore, her funeral was held at that time, and most importantly, it was the exact time of her death.

I hadn't been aware of the last detail, which sent a chill down my spine. Looking at the old clock again, I felt a strange sense of comfort mixed with intrigue.

Since then, the old clock has remained in my living room. Its former ugliness doesn't bother me anymore. It continues to chime four times at 4:00 PM and 4:00 AM. Each chime reminds me of Aunt Barbara, and I like to believe it's her way of saying hello from the other side.

From the Author

I hope you enjoyed my first collection of original ghost experiences and the vast array of phenomena reported by the witnesses. If you would like to submit an experience or was a witness to some of the stories in this book, please email mj@mjwayland.com

For further ghost stories and research as well as my future releases please visit my website - www.mjwayland.com

Thank you

MJ Wayland

My other books include:
50 Real Ghost Stories
50 Real Ghost Stories 2
30 Real Christmas Ghost Stories
50 Real American Ghost Stories
The York Ghost Walk
The Derby Ghost Walk

All are available from Amazon and other good bookshops.

About the Artist

In this, our third collaboration, I am profoundly grateful to the unparalleled artist, Louise Jeffrey. Her artistry not only ignites the embers of inspiration within me but also graces this book with breathtaking visuals. While a captivating ghost tale can spark the fires of our imagination, the artwork by Louise intensifies the flames, encapsulating the very essence of a spectral encounter.

To immerse yourself further in their mesmerising creations, visit unseely.com or find them on social media under the name 'Unseely'.

Watch out for our next book together!

Sycamore Gap by Louise Jeffrey

Printed in Great Britain
by Amazon